Wayfinding with Dietrich Bonhoeffer

"Privileged to participate in the original *Wayfinding* community, I eagerly endorse this study of Bonhoeffer's resolute faith during Hitler's Third Reich. Written for group discussion, the authors highlight Bonhoeffer's significant moments, bidding readers to self-assess their sacrifice for Christ. As Bonhoeffer 'came to the Bible,' subjecting himself to its scrutiny, we are summoned to read the Bible against ourselves. *Wayfinding* compels 'homesick exiles' to unseat cultural idols for 'cruciform Christianity.' An excellent read!"

—RANDALL A. BOLTINGHOUSE, senior minister, Windsor Road Christian Church

"If you need help navigating the life of faith in Jesus, *Wayfinding with Dietrich Bonhoeffer* is a perfect companion. As Bonhoeffer said, we need the 'witness of a brother' to help us through discouraging and uncertain times. Following his journey allows you to see Bonhoeffer's transformation, and it raises your faith to believe God will work that same transformation in you."

—MERIDITH FOSTER, host of *The Unfolding Podcast*

"This book will strengthen your resolve to follow Christ, resist the easy path, and develop a fresh love for how God speaks through the written and incarnate Word of God. Gain prophetic insight on resisting the Powers at work in our day and recognize if the church is to save her life, she must first be willing to lose it. A timely word from Jonathan King and Joseph Thomas!"

—J. R. WOODWARD, national director, V3 Movement

"*Wayfinding with Dietrich Bonhoeffer* offers a deep look at the life and work of Bonhoeffer, while presenting him in an engaging and accessible way. This book could easily be found both on a podium in a seminary classroom and on a couch in a home hosting a small group. A must read for anyone looking to gain intellectual knowledge of the history of the church, while also personally growing in their relationship with Christ!"

—REV. CARLOS M. VELEZ, Calvary Church, Souderton, PA

"Authors Joe Thomas and Jonathan King, both Dietrich Bonhoeffer aficionados, give a creative look into how to find our way in a culture with deep divisions. Using a metaphor from urban planning called wayfinding, they explore Bonhoeffer's faith journey, ultimately leading him to join a conspiracy to remove Hitler from power. The insights and questions following each chapter allow readers to ponder their own future and tough decisions they may have to make."

—DON FOLLIS, director, Pastor-to-Pastor Initiatives

Wayfinding *with* Dietrich Bonhoeffer

Off the Beaten Path and into the Kingdom

Joseph L. Thomas
and Jonathan D. King

CASCADE *Books* • Eugene, Oregon

WAYFINDING WITH DIETRICH BONHOEFFER
Off the Beaten Path and into the Kingdom

Cascade Books
An Imprint of Wipf and Stock Publishers
199 W. 8th Ave., Suite 3
Eugene, OR 97401

www.wipfandstock.com

PAPERBACK ISBN: 978-1-6667-4953-3
HARDCOVER ISBN: 978-1-6667-4954-0
EBOOK ISBN: 978-1-6667-4955-7

Cataloguing-in-Publication data:

Names: Thomas, Joseph L., author. | King, Jonathan D., author.

Title: Wayfinding with Dietrich Bonhoeffer : off the beaten path and into the kingdom / Joseph L. Thomas and Jonathan D. King.

Description: Eugene, OR: Cascade Books, 2024 | Includes bibliographical references.

Identifiers: ISBN 978-1-6667-4953-3 (paperback) | ISBN 978-1-6667-4954-0 (hardcover) | ISBN 978-1-6667-4955-7 (ebook)

Subjects: LCSH: Bonhoeffer, Dietrich, 1906–1945. | Bonhoeffer, Dietrich, 1906–1945—Influence.

Classification: BX4827.B57 W40 2024 (paperback) | BX4827.B57 (ebook)

VERSION NUMBER 11/05/24

Contents

Preface

From our fifth-story perch, we looked out over the micro-urban skyline of Champaign, Illinois, mulling over ideas for the inaugural group who would encounter the material you now hold in your hands. We were dreaming of new language for a workshop focused on the life of Dietrich Bonhoeffer, searching for fresh nomenclature to imbue our group with identity and purpose. Even the space where we stood—a newly constructed business accelerator venue—beckoned us to take an enterprising step. We hashed through familiar terms in the Christian lexicon—pilgrimage, journey, discipleship, etc.—and then like a lightning bolt it came: *wayfinding.*

Appropriated from the arena of urban planning, "wayfinding" felt fresh, contextual, appropriate. Instantly, we agreed this was the new language we were seeking. Wayfinding as a framework provided the foundation and structure we needed for our journey together through the historical witness of Dietrich Bonhoeffer's life.

Since that day when we agreed upon our wayfinding project, the first "Wayfinding with Dietrich Bonhoeffer" community met at the beginning of 2020, before COVID-19's unfortunate interruption. We produced a podcast by the same name in 2022, and an original play based on the material found in chapter 5 of this book had its debut that same year. Two more wayfinding groups walked through the ideas in this book in 2023, and now we are publishing this book as the capstone project in our "Wayfinding with Dietrich Bonhoeffer" ecosystem.

This book and the wayfinding ecosystem are the offshoots of Life Together House, a ministry in Champaign-Urbana, Illinois committed to life together in Christ for the purpose of invigorating the church and creatively engaging a "world wide awake" (a term we've adapted from Bonhoeffer's "world come of age") with the gospel of Jesus Christ.

We have become quite fond of the concept of wayfinding, and plan to produce subsequent books and resources in which we will look back upon the historical witness of individuals, groups, and movements to discern how they might serve as wayfinders for our lives in the twenty-first century. We believe history matters and we want to share it with you in a fresh, accessible manner. We pray you can engage with these ideas alongside others, and wayfind off the beaten path and into the kingdom of God.

Introduction

Stand at the crossroads and look;
ask for the ancient paths,
ask where the good way is,
and walk in it.

—JEREMIAH 6:16

I am the way and the truth and the life.

—JESUS CHRIST, JOHN 14:6

What we discern in Bonhoeffer's writings, confirmed in a remarkable
way by his life and death, is an authentic witness to Jesus Christ in
relation to the situations in which he found himself. He does not
provide us with ready-made answers for our time, but he does indicate
how we might respond in faithfulness to the gospel. With the proviso
that we do not allow his ideas to become "rusty swords" in our hands,
he provides us with insights . . . which can help us in our task of
bearing witness to the gospel in different contexts.

—JOHN W. DE GRUCHY,
DIETRICH BONHOEFFER: WITNESS TO JESUS CHRIST

1

WE BOTH REMEMBER OUR first respective journeys to Paris, France. Standing in front of the transit system in this foreign city with wide eyes, neither of us had traveled to any such large city, let alone a major city in a foreign country or a city with an intricate public transportation system. Thankfully, this subway system had a map, and we each had French-speaking guides who could help navigate this tangle of urban railways. If it wasn't for this wayfinding system and the wayfinders at our sides, we surely would have been lost.

MODERN WAYFINDING

In the density and complexity of today's physical urban centers, modern wayfinding systems are central to best practices for city planners and critical for the well-being of those who dwell there. Modern wayfinding systems orient and guide city dwellers and travelers with thoughtful, well-planned sensory data and cues. You or I may not be intimately familiar with the ancient art and science of wayfinding on the open seas using the environmental cues of atmospheric phenomena, but we are all likely familiar with wayfinding systems and guides which have helped us navigate the complexities of an unfamiliar city, museum, park, or transit system. Perhaps you have benefited from color-coded path lines on sidewalks, informational signposts at intersections, audio tour guides on a mobile app, separated cycling lanes on busy streets, or a detailed map of an urban rail system. These modern wayfinding encounters are not unlike our experience as followers of Christ in a complex, changing world. Secure in Christ's love, we must access and act upon the spiritual resources available that help us find our way in this life. If we only let him, Christ is our ultimate wayfinder, directing us around this earthly city. That is why we believe wayfinding furnishes our imaginations with fresh language for the journey of following Christ today.

FOLLOWERS OF THE WAY

To be a follower of Jesus Christ is to have a Way-finder. We orient our lives along the path of the one who is *the Way*. The Way is a person—the living, risen Christ. And with his Spirit as our guide, we never travel alone, or without his wisdom for the journey.

Yet, the journey is not easy.

The number of "ways" before us today are prolific. Innumerable well-beaten paths, dead-end streets, and sideshow distractions draw our attention away from our Wayfinder and the path of his kingdom. The landscape is complex; the pitfalls are plentiful. We arrive at intersections, wondering which way to turn. Often, we are not entirely sure where we want to end up. Our freedom is both gift and responsibility. While navigating our world, at times we feel lost, restless, aimless, unsure, discouraged, or encumbered. We languish amidst grief and loss collected along the journey. Like the apostle Paul, we may groan, longing for redemption as we face trials and persecution. But we are invited to imitate his example in the face of adversity—as he imitated Christ—remembering and proclaiming as he did before his persecutors: "I admit that I worship the God of our ancestors as a follower of the Way . . ." (Acts 24:14).

As followers of this Way, we hold in tension the "already" and the "not yet" of our wayfinding *telos*. Our wayfinding *always* has a destination in mind. Because the Way is *already* set before us now but *not yet* fully manifest, we journey as homesick exiles in a foreign land with a cruciform calling to turn off of the beaten path of self-preservation and to join God in "[seeking] the peace and prosperity of the city" where we have been placed (Jer 29:7). Paradoxically, though, we follow the Way that is *already at hand*; we rejoice that we are not alone and that we are invited to participate in the resurrection of his new creation even now.

So, with our feet firmly planted on the earth and our eyes fixed on the risen and reigning Christ, we journey here as ones who pray and labor toward that future city. We bear witness here and now to the good news with our words and our actions, even as we set our hope upon the resurrection when God comes to dwell with us, and we reign with Christ in his renewed heavens and earth.

With this vision before us, we need companions and the encouragement of faithful guides—wayfinders—to aid us in our various contexts, challenges, and circumstances. The writer of Hebrews exhorts us to recall the cloud of witnesses who have gone before us, the lives of the faithful who echo through history, reminding us too that "here we do not have an enduring city, but we are looking for the city that is to come" (Heb 13:14).

WAYFINDING TODAY

We believe Dietrich Bonhoeffer is one such wayfinder for us today. Bonhoeffer's particular testimony and witness invite us to follow Christ alone as the true Way, and to do so with trusted companions while we sojourn amidst enemies, evil, and adversity. Bonhoeffer both embodied and proclaimed this wisdom that we need fellow sojourners on the Way:

> God has willed that we should seek and find his living Word in the witness of a brother, in the mouth of man. Therefore, the Christian needs another Christian who speaks God's Word to him. He needs him again and again when he becomes uncertain and discouraged, for by himself he cannot help himself without belying the truth. He needs his brother as a bearer and proclaimer of the divine word of salvation.[1]

So, with the witness of a faithful forerunner such as Bonhoeffer and the fellowship of one another, let us walk the Way together with perseverance, humility, conviction, and hearts eager to learn from the wisdom of faithful ones who've traveled before us.

WHAT YOU'LL FIND IN THIS BOOK

We wish to let Bonhoeffer's life speak for itself and invite you, the reader, to journey with us to observe the complex landscape of his life and discern the wayfinding cues that help guide us along the Way today. We expect this book will help you weave together the past, present, and future of Bonhoeffer's life and yours—to inhabit time with faithfulness to the witness of the past, intentionality and wisdom in the present, and vision for a future as a more mature follower of Christ (see Figure 1 for an illustration of how this book will aid you as a disciple of Jesus Christ). We will remember we are not to live isolated lives caught up in the ephemerality of today's attention economy, nor are we to be so focused on the future that we are no earthly good, but rather we are to situate ourselves among the great cloud of witnesses and faithfully incarnate the faith we've inherited.

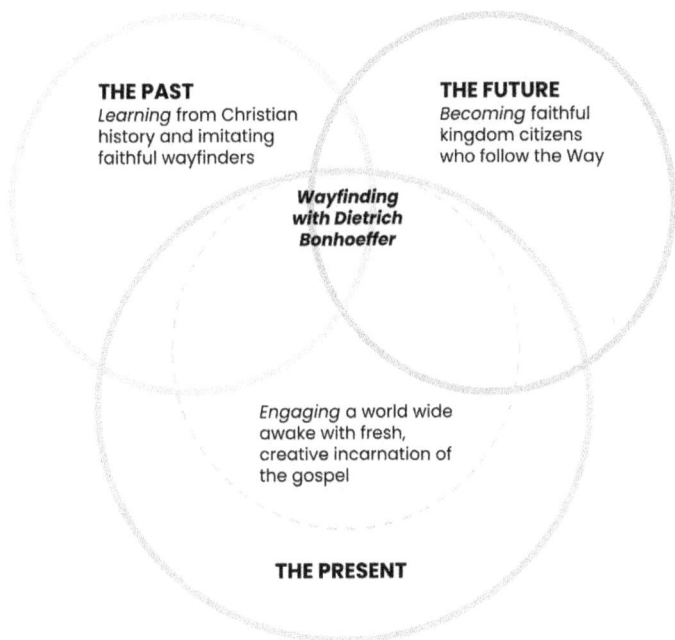

THE PAST
Learning from Christian history and imitating faithful wayfinders

THE FUTURE
Becoming faithful kingdom citizens who follow the Way

Wayfinding with Dietrich Bonhoeffer

Engaging a world wide awake with fresh, creative incarnation of the gospel

THE PRESENT

There are six chapters in this book, each a reflection upon a theme drawn from Bonhoeffer's life. We will look at the phenomena of his life, traveling with him off the beaten path to consider six uniquely significant themes of his life and writings—themes which are not commonly known by readers already acquainted with his popular works and popular biographies (e.g., *Discipleship* and *Life Together*). This is not to dismiss the significance of other themes, writings, or significant moments in Bonhoeffer's life (e.g., his influential year in New York and Harlem), but to travel with him on a more unexpected journey to spur thoughtful reflection upon Bonhoeffer's choices at different junctures. What do we think about his words and his decision in a particular place and time?

Finally, each chapter concludes with "Wayfinding Cues" that help distill our reflections from the chapter to help you stand back and review the wayfinding observations of Bonhoeffer's life. You will also find "Wayfinding Questions" to guide you further into a space of reflection and action, ideally alongside a community of fellow travelers who wish to avoid the beaten path and follow the Way. We encourage you to also follow along with our companion podcast, "Wayfinding," which will help you go further with the content in this study.

1

Paths of Resistance[2]

WITHIN MONTHS OF HIS appointment as reich chancellor of Germany on January 30, 1933, Adolf Hitler set in motion a policy of *Gleichschaltung*, loosely translated, "coordination." Audacious in its concept and breathtaking in its reach, this policy of coordination sought to bring every part of German society into alignment with the Nazi regime's racial and nationalist views.

By July of that year, the effort to establish the policy of coordination could be declared an unmitigated success. Nearly every government entity and public and private institution, including voluntary organizations, had come into alignment. Many came enthusiastically as new converts to the *Weltanschauung* of blood, soil, and race—the worship of the *Volk*—while others submitted through fear or for self-preservation. Opponents of the policy who had the means, talent, foresight, and connections to flee to other countries did so. Less fortunate opponents were either shot or interned in the first concentration camps. By August 1934, when the German military forces swore a

> **Weltanschauung**
> A particular philosophy or view of life; the worldview of an individual or group.

personal oath of loyalty to Adolf Hitler, the coordination of the German nation was almost complete.

Almost. Only the church remained to be co-opted.

A small coterie of Christians dared to resist Nazi coordination through the creation of the Confessing Church. At the forefront of this group, and among its most zealous defenders, stood the Lutheran pastor Dietrich Bonhoeffer. Twenty-seven years old when the policy of *Gleichschaltung* was first enacted, Bonhoeffer spent the rest of the 1930s rousing the church, inside and outside of Germany, to speak a divine word and take action against Nazi fanaticism and the "German Christians," National Socialist sycophants dressed up as Christians. Bonhoeffer displayed an unusual nimbleness as he experimented with the best means of peaceful resistance. He first looked outward to the ecumenical movement, then began flirting with Gandhian ideas of peaceful resistance, and finally turned inward to concentrate on the formation of the spiritual resources necessary to sustain the Confessing Church under persecution.

Volk

Simply, "people." Under the Nazis, it took on a richer meaning denoting "race" that is tied to a particular place or "land" that provides a mystical meaning about the greatness and superiority of these people, specifically, the Nordic people of northern Europe.

Indefatigable in his efforts to save the church and defeat the principalities and powers of racism, militarism, and jingoism, Bonhoeffer resisted to the end of a noose, where he died at the hands of Nazi henchmen in 1945. Yet, as the Scriptures teach, a seed cannot bear fruit unless it falls to the ground and dies. And so, all would not be lost at the gallows, nor victory ungrasped, as the life and writings of this saint would go on to inspire future generations of Christians to resist the evil in their day. In the inscrutable judgment of the Lord of history, success would finally come to this Christian of resistance.

ECUMENICAL CHURCH RESISTANCE

From the outset, Bonhoeffer possessed an unusual prophetic sensitivity to the evil overtures emanating from the Nazi movement. Even as the National Socialists were still accumulating power in the Reichstag, he was calling on the ecumenical movement to speak a "divine word" against the rising militarism they represented. Bonhoeffer firmly believed in the power embedded in Jesus' Sermon on the Mount to resist evil and establish peace. "Here alone [in the Sermon on the Mount] lies the force that can blow all this hocus-pocus sky-high—like fireworks," he wrote.[3] If the "heathens" in the east—a reference to Gandhi and his followers—could grasp the shape and power of Jesus' teachings to world-changing effect, surely the church of Jesus Christ could counter the "misleader" (*Verführer*), Bonhoeffer's wordplay on Hitler's self-designation as *der Führer*.

der Führer
Simply, "leader."
Under the Nazis it came
to mean the rise of a
messianic figure who
would lead Germany to
greatness, i.e., Adolf Hitler.

Bonhoeffer urged the World Alliance for Promoting Fellowship through the Churches—a multi-national ecumenical group of Protestant churches—to issue a proclamation against militarism. In his speech "The Church and the Peoples of the World," he called upon the ecumenical body to speak a "divine word" to an unsettled world, choosing Psalm 85 as his biblical text: "I will hear what God the Lord will speak: for he will speak peace unto his people, and to his saints."[4] He implored the World Alliance to consider itself a "Church Council," an unprecedented idea.

Even before Germany fired the first salvo against the Jews Bonhoeffer promulgated a new conciliar understanding of Protestantism that could speak authoritatively to the nation of Germany, indeed to all warring nations:

conciliar
a theological term
referencing a church
council that makes
theological decisions
for the church.

> When will it be that Christianity says the right word at the right time. . . . Only the one great Ecumenical Council of the Holy Church of Christ over all the world can speak out so that the world, though it gnash its teeth, will have to hear, so that the peoples will rejoice because the Church of Christ in the name of Christ has taken the weapons from the hands of their sons, forbidden war, and proclaimed the peace of Christ against the raging world . . . There is no way to peace along the way of safety. For peace must be dared.[5]

Like so many other efforts he made to rouse the church to rise up and act, the "divine word" he called for was never delivered. A couple of resolutions was the best the World Alliance could muster.

CONFESSING CHURCH RESISTANCE

On the heels of the Nazi party's ascension to power came the emergence of the "German Christian" movement. Dedicated to replacing everything Jewish within the Christian faith, the "German Christians" sought to conform Christianity to Nazi ideology. Their first move was to implement the "Aryan Paragraph," a piece of legislation ordering the removal of all Jewish-Christian pastors who had not served in the First World War. Bonhoeffer recognized immediately that the Aryan Paragraph was a direct attack on the very foundations of the Christian faith. As a result, he called for a *status confessionis*—an idea in Lutheranism that traced its origins back to the sixteenth century—which declares that a certain issue is admissible of only one proper interpretation in the church. The declaration of a *status confessionis* could be made if a new tenet of faith was ruled to be antithetical to the theological and doctrinal integrity of the church.

ideology
a system of ideas and ideals, especially one which forms the basis of economic or political theory and policy.

By the end of 1934, Bonhoeffer—along with Martin Niemoller and Karl Barth—had helped guide opponents of the

"German Christians" into the Confessing Church. Based on his call for a *status confessionis,* Bonhoeffer argued that the Confessing Church was *the church* in Germany, declaring the Reich Church a heretical ecclesiastical body: "Whoever knowingly cuts himself off from the Confessing Church in Germany cuts himself off from salvation."[6] He envisioned the Confessing Church as a base from which to resist Nazi ideology—specifically its anti-Semitism—and to prevent the church's complete "coordination."

Yet he foresaw that many who adhered to the Confessing Church at the outset would not remain in the fight when it intensified. With allusions to Hebrews 12:4, he began to speak of eventual martyrdom for Christian resisters:

> And while I'm working with the church opposition with all my might, it's perfectly clear to me that this opposition is only a very temporary transitional phase on the way to an opposition of a very different kind, and that very few of those involved in this preliminary skirmish are going to be there for that second struggle. I believe that all of Christendom should be praying with us for the coming of resistance "to the point of shedding of blood" and for the finding of people who can suffer it through.[7]

SERMON ON THE MOUNT RESISTANCE

In 1935, the Confessing Church invited Bonhoeffer to develop and lead a seminary. But what kind of Christian seminary should be built? Bonhoeffer was still trying to determine the best church response to the Nazi regime. Should a traditional seminary be formed for the preparation of Lutheran pastors, or was something more needed in this dire time of "German Christians" and Nazi overlords? Should a Christian community be formed that would look more like a Gandhian ashram, existing for the express purpose of leading a nonviolent movement to overthrow Hitler and his followers? Three years earlier he had lectured, "[The church] was destined to be, instead, the community of Jesus Christ that is within the world, yet free enough from the world to oppose secular ideologies and to do the courageous deeds required in serving others."[8]

With these thoughts swirling in his head, he asked the Anglican priest C. F. Andrews, a confidant of Gandhi, to write a letter of introduction to the Indian leader. Gandhi's Satyagraha movement of peaceful resistance against British colonialism in India found inspiration in Jesus' teachings in the Sermon on the Mount. Might something similar be attainable in Nazi Germany? "If Pastor Bonhoeffer comes to India to enquire about what is being done for World Peace through Ahimsa and Satyagraha, I do hope you will be able to see him," Andrews wrote.[9]

Bonhoeffer also wrote to Gandhi, expressing his plans for the church as a point of leverage against Nazism: "Only Christianity can help our western peoples to a new and spiritually sound life... But Christianity must be something very different from what it has become in these days... Western Christianity must be reborn as the Sermon on the Mount."[10] Bonhoeffer sought to learn the tactics of resistance Gandhi had developed so that Western Christians could "learn from you what realisation of faith means, what life devoted to political and racial peace means."[11] He dreamed of forming a new type of pastor who could awaken those abiding comfortably in their "justified" church pews. "Following Christ—what that really is, I'd like to know—it is not exhausted by our concept of faith," he wrote from London to his friend and interlocutor Erwin Sutz as he struggled to find the right path forward.[12]

But Bonhoeffer soon discarded Gandhi's approach, recognizing its impracticability in confronting Hitler. Gandhi's nonviolent tactics were predicated on the assumption that the oppressor could be shamed, shown his hypocrisy, and forced through public pressure to live up to his ideals. The British believed they were operating on Christian principles for the uplift and betterment of the Indian people. When it was made clear—after many protests, boycotts, and physical blows—that their policies were missing the mark and were rejected by most Indians, the British reversed course and eventually left India.

None of this was possible with Hitler, Bonhoeffer realized. Like all totalizing ideologies, Nazism was about converting people—and using force where this failed. More than one German of high standing approached Hitler believing he could change the Führer and his inner circle of ideologues. It never happened. When Bonhoeffer heard that the Christian leader Frank Buchanan, head of the Oxford Group, sought a personal audience with Hitler, he scoffed, "The Oxford movement was naive enough to try and convert Hitler—a ridiculous failure to recognize what is going on. We are the ones to be converted, not Hitler."[13]

DISCIPLESHIP AS RESISTANCE

Bonhoeffer soon turned away from thoughts of creating peace activists to the idea of forming pastors capable of leading their congregations into resistance against the allure of Nazi anti-Jewish and nationalistic propaganda, pastors who could follow Christ "to the point of the shedding of blood."[14] His perspective on the Sermon on the Mount turned from being the inspiration for the creation of a world-changing social movement to being the inspiration for the formation of pastors who would be able to persevere in a time of persecution. His most popular book, *The Cost of Discipleship*, came out of this context.

Bonhoeffer believed the key to church survival must be found in developing the right spiritual resources in church leaders. Pastors steeped in spiritual disciplines could best be formed in a quasi-monastic setting where daily meditation, Bible study, and worship were emphasized. He designed a new seminary at Finkenwalde around these spiritual lodestars.

After his other efforts to develop Christian resistance in Nazi Germany, it was in the creation of Finkenwalde that Bonhoeffer found his footing. Discipleship became the key; obedience to Christ's commands was the only sure road to resistance; faith was the catalyst. Only this approach could create the spiritual armor needed to resist Hitler's evangelizing message of racial superiority.

Daily meditation on the Scriptures was the foundation. Bonhoeffer knew whereof he spoke. During his time at Finkenwalde, he reflected on earlier days when personal ambition reigned in his life. In a 1936 letter to his former classmate, Elisabeth Zinn, he wrote:

> I threw myself into my work in an extremely un-Christian and not at all humble fashion. . . It was quite bad. But then something different came, something that has changed and transformed my life to this very day. For the first time, I came to the Bible . . . I was not yet a Christian but rather in an utterly wild and uncontrolled fashion my own master . . . The Bible, especially the Sermon on the Mount, freed me from all this . . . Then came the crisis of 1933. This strengthened me in it.[15]

Bonhoeffer taught his ordinands that daily Bible reading and memorization were the most crucial spiritual resources they possessed. He implored them to let "no day of our life in office . . . go past without our having read the Bible."[16] Not only would this discipline safeguard the pastors against the fiery arrows of Nazi propaganda, but it would also help ground their decisions in the Word of God. Bonhoeffer had complained to Sutz as early as 1933 that in regard to the "Jewish question" even "the most intelligent people have totally lost both their heads and their Bible."[17]

And there was something else. Scripture memorization would be indispensable to the pastors' very survival if they were placed in prison without their Bibles. "We know that it was quite a long time before some of the brothers who were arrested were given Bibles," he wrote. "Weeks like that can prove whether we have been faithful in our reading of Scripture and whether in our knowledge of Scripture we have acquired a great treasury."[18]

For the purposes of meditation, he turned to the *Moravian Daily Text*, a devotional book he had used since childhood. As the Finkenwalde community was dispersed and its students sent to isolated pastorates, prison, and, later, the front lines of the war, Bonhoeffer reminded them to meditate each day on the *Daily Texts*. His circular letters to his former Finkenwalde students— masterpieces of pastoral care—encouraged them to stand strong in their difficult circumstances. Christians belong "in the midst of enemies. There they find their mission, their work," he told them.[19] And regular meditation on the *Daily Texts*, especially when they were separated from each other, "keeps us in the saving fellowship of the community, the brethren, our spiritual home."[20]

While the Word of God was the ground of the Finkenwalde discipleship regiment, Bonhoeffer also emphasized the importance of music—a spiritual resource that had been a trustworthy balm of Gilead during the trials of his own journey. And so, he made it a mandatory part of life at Finkenwalde. In a report written in 1936, he noted, "Now as before, we spend a great deal of time and derive great joy from our music making . . . in general, I can hardly imagine our life together here without our daily music making. We have driven out many an evil spirit in this way."[21] The brothers would find this to be even more true as they were driven into extraordinary situations that tested their resolve and commitment. In one memorable lecture given during the 1936 Berlin Olympic Games, Bonhoeffer told his hearers, "The ancient Christians were still singing even as they were being thrown to the lions."[22]

RESISTANCE CONTINUED

Was it all for nothing? Even though his many futile efforts to rouse the church to action left Bonhoeffer frustrated, he never fell into despair. In his final years in prison he imagined a future where Jesus' words would fall afresh on new ears with the same arresting power as when Jesus first spoke them:

> The day will come . . . when people will once more be called to speak the word of God in such a way that the world is changed and renewed. It will be in a new language, perhaps quite nonreligious language, but liberating and redeeming like Jesus' language, so that people will be alarmed, and yet overcome by its power—the language of a new righteousness and truth, a language proclaiming that God makes peace with humankind and that God's kingdom is drawing near.[23]

Bonhoeffer was not to see a successful church resistance movement rise up against Nazi Germany. But what did not happen in his lifetime came to fruition after his death.

The legacy of his words and actions helped the church in East Germany to persevere and to create a form of resistance that ultimately witnessed the collapse of the communist regime there. What began as a prayer service in Leipzig during the early 1980s ended in the Candlelight Revolution, which brought millions of Germans out from under the yoke of communism in 1989. Not long afterward, the world witnessed the amazing reunion of West and East Germany. Bonhoeffer himself had envisioned the church someday leading the nations in reconciliation:

> The "justification and renewal" of the West, therefore, will come only when justice, order, and peace are in one way or another restored, when past guilt is thereby "forgiven," when it is no longer imagined that what has been done can be undone by means of punitive measures and reprisals, and when the church of Jesus Christ, as the fountainhead of all forgiveness, justification, and renewal, is given room to do its work among the nations.[24]

Good fruit can be garnered from Bonhoeffer's insights, experiences, and example of resistance in our own day as well, a time when political ideologies are trying to bring the church into "coordination" through cultural pressure, political enticement, and, increasingly, riotous intimidation. Suffice it to say there are ill winds blowing through our civilization.

Recognizing the "cost of discipleship" and making efforts to inculcate the spiritual resources necessary to survive in an increasingly hostile climate seem more pertinent than ever. In this situation, we must find our mission and work "in the midst of enemies," as Bonhoeffer put it.[25]

Dietrich Bonhoeffer's words about Jesus Christ remain potent today. He would not seek credit for himself but, instead, point people to the Lord: "Christ alone adjures the false gods and the demons. Only before the cross does the world tremble, not before us."[26]

WAYFINDING CUES

The following wayfinding cues from Dietrich Bonhoeffer's life and thought can help us navigate the unsettled times in which we live. Bonhoeffer's witness has been a spiritual resource for many, including the church in communist East Germany, and the church in South Africa. We offer these wayfinding cues to help the reader glean insights and lessons that wayfinding with Dietrich Bonhoeffer presents. Like him, we seek to leave the beaten path in our culture and enter the kingdom of Christ among us today.

- The Church in Germany faced two major challenges under the Nazi regime: the temptation to commingle the gospel of Jesus Christ with a political ideology and the lure of a charismatic political leader to fix their nation's social and economic problems.

- Early on, Dietrich Bonhoeffer discerned the Confessing Church's conflict with Nazism to be as much a spiritual battle as a contest between differing human viewpoints.

- Through the ecumenical movement, a call for a *status confessionis*, and the use of nonviolent direct actions, Bonhoeffer urged the church to use its influence and social standing with the German people to combat the militarism of the Nazis.

- The formation of the seminary at Finkenwalde sought to train pastors for the dark days ahead through deep Bible study and memorization, a daily life of practicing the spiritual disciplines, and making worship central to the Christian life.

WAYFINDING QUESTIONS

1. This chapter describes the "principalities and powers" that Bonhoeffer and the Confessing Church faced in Nazi Germany. What were they?

2. Bonhoeffer explored many different approaches to confronting the Nazi regime. Can you name them?

3. Why do you think Bonhoeffer found his footing at Finkenwalde?

4. What spiritual resources did Bonhoeffer try to develop in his seminarians?

5. Why were these spiritual resources necessary?

6. What future hope did Bonhoeffer envision for the church and the proclamation of the gospel?

DEEP WAYFINDING

1. As Christians how can we recognize a false ideology, one that runs counter to the teachings of Christ and the Scriptures?

2. How do we prevent fear from driving us into the arms of a political "strong man"?

2

Paths Through the Bible

HIS EARLY YEARS

EACH PERSON HAS A unique story about how they began to follow Jesus Christ. It is no different with Dietrich Bonhoeffer. For him, the Christian life only became a reality once he discovered the paradigm-shifting power of the Scriptures. "Discovered" might seem like an odd word choice for a pastor, theologian, and ethicist, but the truth is, Bonhoeffer knew the husk of the Bible long before he encountered the kernel of the radical gospel message of Jesus Christ. The intellectual rigor of his theological education prepared him well to peer down the different labyrinths of textual studies and engage the philosophical discussions of his day; to set him up on the career path of a professor and scholar. Yet about the life behind the Bible, the sort of spiritual power that transforms lives and communities, he remained ignorant. For Bonhoeffer, the letters on the pages took time to ripen into the Word of God.

Instead, early on Bonhoeffer used the Scriptures like any other book—as a means to advance his career and engage his intellectual curiosity. To provide a platform for his voice to be heard, and make him an academic prodigy, an up-and-coming university recruit.

His future was a bright one, and though the path before him required much work, it was also clear and predictable. Someone as talented as Bonhoeffer could navigate it on his own strength. Not at this time in his life was he—as he said later—reading the Bible against himself. Rather, the Bible was the means to fulfill his personal ambitions and satisfy his ego. This may be difficult for twenty-first–century Westerners to understand. During the time when Bonhoeffer lived, being a pastor or theologian was a highly respected position. So, it was not a great leap for someone with Bonhoeffer's ambitions to move up in society, or make a name for themselves, through the church. Bonhoeffer sums up best his own unruly vanity at this time, in a letter to his friend Elisabeth Zinn on January 27, 1936:

> I threw myself into my work in an extremely un-Christian and not at all humble fashion. A rather crazy element of ambition . . . It was quite bad . . . I had often preached, I had seen a great deal of the church, had spoken and written about it—and yet I was not yet a Christian but rather in an utterly wild and uncontrolled fashion my own master. I do know that at the time I turned the cause of Jesus Christ into an advantage for myself, for my crazy vanity. I pray to God that will never happen again. Nor had I ever prayed, or had done so only very rarely. Despite this isolation, I was quite happy with myself.[27]

TURNING TOWARD REALITY THROUGH THE BIBLE

Sometime during his year of study in America (1930–31) and thereafter Bonhoeffer began to read the Bible as the Word of God. If not quite a conversion, as his Lutheran pietistic influences might define it, this new direction confirmed a path away from his personal ego toward Jesus Christ. A rather oblique comment in 1944 was the most he would reveal on this change in his life: "It was then that I turned from phraseology to reality."[28]

Henceforth, he sought to hear God's divine word—especially as it related to the church. In a London sermon from 1933, he surely spoke autobiographically when he preached:

> . . . to repent, therefore, means to be in this process of turning around, turning around away from our own accomplishments and receiving God's mercy. Turn back, turn back! The whole Bible calls to us joyfully. Turn back—where? To the everlasting mercy of the God who never leaves us, whose heart breaks because of us, the God who created us and loves us beyond all measure. God will be merciful—so come then, Judgment Day. Lord Jesus, make us ready. We await you with joy. Amen.[29]

Or even more personally put, he once enjoined his students to remember "that we should not forget that every word of Holy Scriptures was a quite personal message of God's love for us."[30] And then he asked them whether they "loved Jesus." During these critical years of the pre-Nazi period, Bonhoeffer came to know Christ more intimately.

Pietism

a seventeenth-century spiritual renewal movement that emphasized heart conversion, small group Bible study, and church action to help the poor.

LIBERATED BY SCRIPTURE

So, what occurred during the time surrounding his 1930–31 year in America?

First, as a student at Union Theological Seminary in New York, Bonhoeffer met the African American Frank Fisher, who invited him to join him at the Abyssinian Church in Harlem. Bonhoeffer soon became a mainstay at the church, eventually teaching Sunday school. His immersion into American Black spirituality moved and changed him. He even brought some vinyl records of Black spirituals to the seminary at Finkenwalde, perplexing his German seminarians to no end. The reception of the preached

Word by the Black congregation helped Bonhoeffer discover the dynamic power of the cross of Christ and the life-changing power of God's Word, not merely the academic phraseology to which he was accustomed.

Second, fellow Union classmate Jean Laserre also left a lasting impression on Bonhoeffer. Laserre was a French pacifist who challenged the German Bonhoeffer to reconsider the meaning and practical application of the Sermon on the Mount for today. They even went to the movie house together to watch *All Quiet on the Western Front*, a moving film for Bonhoeffer that amplified the anti-war sentiment gaining momentum after the devastation of the First World War.

Fisher and Laserre were the equivalent of a left jab and right knockout punch to the self-satisfied Bonhoeffer. Specifically, for Bonhoeffer, these two student encounters during his time at Union Seminary in New York City drew his attention to the teachings of Jesus Christ as found in the Sermon on the Mount, which worked to shatter his self-promoting ego:

> The Bible, especially the Sermon on the Mount, freed me from all this. Since then everything has changed. I have felt this plainly and so have other people around me. That was a great liberation. It became clear to me that the life of a servant of Jesus Christ must belong to the church, and step-by-step it became clearer to me how far it must go. Then came the crisis of 1933. This strengthened me in it.[31]

From this influential year in New York, Bonhoeffer explains his sudden change of perspective on the Bible in startling terms: "But then something different came, something that has changed and transformed my life to this very day. For the first time, I came to the Bible. That, too, is an awful thing to say."[32]

"I came to the Bible"—what an enigmatic statement. What did it mean? On one hand, the Scriptures liberated Bonhoeffer from himself—more exactly, from the iron hold his ego had over his life. On the other hand, biblical liberation inexorably directed him to a life of servanthood. Martin Luther described in his 1520 pamphlet *On Christian Liberty* his own paradoxical life-changing encounter with the full force of the Word of God: "A Christian is a perfectly free lord of all, subject to none. A Christian is a perfectly dutiful servant of all, subject of all."[33]

HOW TO READ THE BIBLE

With this liberated view of the Bible, Bonhoeffer became a fervent advocate for the life-changing capacity of the Word of God. In 1936, he wrote a letter to his brother-in-law, Rudiger Schleicher, instructing him how to read the Scriptures profitably. This letter offers the clearest insight into Bonhoeffer's understanding of the power-changing force of the Scriptures when rightly engaged and read. Not just another book, nor any sort of book, but rather the potential of God's very words to change a person's reality are found within the Bible:

textual criticism
the scientific study of the numerous ancient Greek and Latin scriptural manuscripts upon which we base our Bible translations.

> One cannot simply read the Bible like other books. One must really be prepared to put questions to it. . . . his reason for this is that in the Bible God speaks to us. And one cannot just proceed to think about God under one's own steam; instead, one must ask God questions. Think of how we come to understand something said to us by a person we love not by dissecting it into bits but by simply accepting it as the kind of word it is, so that for days it echoes within us simply as the word of that particular person whom we love; the more we, like Mary, "ponder it in the heart," the more the person who has said it to us becomes accessible to us in the word. That is just how we should treat the word of the Bible . . . I also want to say to you now by way of an entirely personal note, that since I learned to read the Bible in this way—which is by no means such a long time ago—it has become more wonderful to me every day.[34]

Reading the Bible Requires Practice

It was Bonhoeffer's persistent exhortation, before his students, fellow pastors, and the church at large, to pursue disciplined practice when it came to the Christian life. There would be no following of Christ without the discipline of daily reading the Scriptures. Bonhoeffer referred to this, along with worship and prayer, as the "arcane discipline."[35] Like an athlete preparing for a big game, the Christian must hone his body and mind for the contests that lie ahead. The Spirit leads best through a mind sharpened by hours of study over the Word of God. When he taught his 1932–33 courses at the University of Berlin, he made sure to emphasize the art of listening to the Scriptures as much as digging into the text as a scholar.

In 1934 he wrote to his good friend Erwin Sutz, "I am busy with a work that I would like to call exercises."[36] Two books emerged out of this period of intense concentration and experimentation on the role of the spiritual disciplines in the life of the individual Christian and Christian community: *Life Together* and *The Cost of Discipleship*. Both emphasized the central role of the Scriptures in the life of the believer and the church. Followers of Christ must have a ready knowledge of the Bible so that they can encourage their fellow Christians in times of deep trouble and anguish:

> God has willed that we should seek and find His living Word in the witness of a brother, in the mouth of man. Therefore, the Christian needs another Christian who speaks God's Word to him. He needs him again and again when he becomes uncertain and discouraged, for by himself he cannot help himself without belying the truth. He needs his brother as a bearer and proclaimer of the divine word of salvation. He needs his brother solely because of Jesus Christ. The Christ in his own heart is weaker than the Christ in the word of his brother; his own heart is uncertain, his brother's is sure.[37]

It takes time and work to create a storehouse of biblical understanding that leads to such deep fellowship. But how else can we speak God's Word to each other unless we know it? And how can we know it unless we read and study it? "Practice" is Bonhoeffer's watchword. In his book *Creation and Fall*, Bonhoeffer admonished his readers on the need to take one more step beyond reading and study of the Scriptures, and that was to live it. Practice involved all three endeavors—reading, studying, living—and the Christian life was incomplete for Bonhoeffer if any one part was neglected:

> One can never hear it [the Bible], if one does not at the same time live it—and this involves especially *exercitium* [practice]. For us the word of God always lies hidden like a treasure in a field, for we always have to come to the knowledge of God via the cross of Christ.[38]

READY AND WATCHING WITH THE WORD OF GOD

A Christian disciplined in the practice of a full devotional life is ready for hard times when they come. The Confessing Church did not have to wait long for the Nazi regime to crack down on their religious liberty. Bonhoeffer's admonishment to his fellow pastors to be ready, beyond reading and memorizing the Scriptures by heart, proved prescient. Bonhoeffer's warning echoes for us today:

> No day of our life in office may go past without our having read the Bible on it. The controversies of the last months have once again clearly shown to our shame how unversed in Holy Scripture we still are . . . Indeed, how little did people so often listen when the Bible was read out, and how readily did they swallow all the novelties. This must be changed. We must make it a rule to look for scriptural evidence of every decision that confronts us, and not to rest until we have found it. Our confidence in dealing with the Bible must increase year by year. And there is something else. We know that it was quite a long time before some of the brothers who were arrested were given Bibles. Weeks like that can prove whether we have been faithful in our reading of Scripture and whether in our knowledge of Scripture we have acquired a great treasury.[39]

Only the Bible provides us with the confidence to make decisions as they relate to the complex issues of the church and instructs us on how we should live today in an evil world. Otherwise, we find ourselves drowning in our own ideas and trapped in our thinking. Bonhoeffer recognized how easily corrupted our own thinking could become; how easy it was for the ideologies of this world, through the principalities and powers, to co-opt our thought and take us captive: "How readily did they swallow all the novelties," to quote Bonhoeffer again.[40] Only the Word of God can counteract the vain philosophies of this world, can conquer them, and set our minds upon the wisdom and knowledge of God.

principalities and powers the Bible speaks of the reality of unseen forces with the ability to influence us individually and societally.

But this does not come to us through some sort of spiritual osmosis. We must practice if we are to be ready for the battles we encounter in this world. So Bonhoeffer admonishes:

> We must once again get to know the Scriptures as the reformers and our forebears knew them. We must not shy away from the work and the time required for this task. We must become acquainted with the Scriptures first and foremost for the sake of our salvation. But, besides this, there are enough weighty reasons to make this challenge absolutely urgent for us. For example, how are we ever to gain certainty and confidence in our personal deeds and church activity if we do not stand on solid biblical ground? It is not our heart that determines our course, but God's Word. But who in this day has any proper awareness of the need for evidence from Scripture? How often do we hear innumerable arguments "from life" and "from experience" to justify the most crucial decisions? Yet the evidence of Scripture is excluded even though it would perhaps point in exactly the opposite direction.[41]

We too often prefer our own thoughts to the Scriptures, and because we do not practice learning the Bible we are often only left with our own thoughts. And then we wonder what went wrong.

This is the way that leads to deep troubles. This is how we are co-opted by wrong thinking and ideologies that stray from the path of Scripture. Intelligence does not matter. Bonhoeffer was astounded as some of the most intelligent people he knew embraced the Nazi party and anti-Jewish propaganda. It caused him to remark that "the most intelligent people have totally lost both their heads and their Bible."[42]

Instead, Bonhoeffer proposed a deep wrestling with the Word of God. Not being satisfied with our first read of the scriptural passage, we must press on to ever deeper reflection. This is not just a pastoral task. Every Christian is called to study the Scriptures energetically—to practice:

> I need time for God's word and often have to ponder the words for a long time in order to understand the precepts of God correctly. Nothing would be more mistaken than that kind of activity or sentimentality that devalues pondering and reflection. It is also a matter not only for those especially called to this but for everyone who wants to walk in God's ways.[43]

BRIEF EXCURSUS ON BONHOEFFER'S THEOLOGICAL VIEW OF THE SCRIPTURES

It is important to clear up any confusion about Bonhoeffer's views of the Bible. At least one conservative critic makes the argument that Bonhoeffer was indeed a theological "liberal," and many liberal theologians seek to claim him as one of their own.[44] Specifically, some point to his response to Rudolf Bultmann to support this claim. Is this the case?

The publication of Bultmann's *New Testament and Mythology: The Problem of Demythologizing the New Testament Message* created a sensation in the theological world of 1941. The premise of the theological essay was to demythologize the story of Christ, clearing out all supernatural elements from the life and teaching of Jesus to make Christ more acceptable to the modern mind. The timing of his writing in 1941 caused the Confessing Church, of which Bultmann was a member, to wrestle with his possible expulsion from their ranks. Bonhoeffer defended Bultmann's right as a scholar to publish what he wanted and even believed that some of his ideas might be useful to making Christianity more non-religious—a pursuit of Bonhoeffer's during his prison years. It is the selective use of these positive comments regarding Bultmann which have led some scholars to declare Bonhoeffer a liberal.

But reading the positive comments in context quickly dispels any notion that Bonhoeffer was attracted to Bultmann's demythologizing approach or to liberal, early twentieth-century Christian theology in general. We have two examples for consideration. First, Bonhoeffer wrote to Winfried Krause, a student at Finkenwalde, in 1942, "Now as to Bultmann: I belong to those who welcomed his writing—not because I agree with it . . . I would like to speak with Bultmann about this and open myself to the fresh air that comes from him. But then the window has to be shut again. Otherwise, the susceptible will too easily catch a cold."[45] And, secondly, to Ernst Wolf, German theologian and member of the Confessing Church, later in 1942, he wrote, "If the same thing happened here [expulsion of Bultmann], I think I would have to have myself expelled as well, not because I agree with Bultmann, but because I consider the other's attitude by far more dangerous than Bultmann's."[46]

No one should be surprised that Bonhoeffer sought to protect Bultmann on the grounds of academic freedom. Indeed, Bultmann's publication appeared during one of the most repressive regimes in history. Bonhoeffer himself had been banned from entering Berlin, preaching, and publication. There was a natural empathy there. And one should never forget that Bonhoeffer was the son and brother of academics. Still, his letters leave no doubt that Bonhoeffer disapproved of Bultmann's views on the supernatural elements of Jesus' life. In a letter to Bethge he makes this plain: "My view, however, is that the full content, including the "mythological" concepts, must remain—the New Testament is not a mythological dressing up of a universal truth, but this mythology (resurrection and so forth) is the thing itself!"[47] Contrary to Bultmann, Bonhoeffer boldly proclaimed the resurrection to be historically true.

Finally, it is true Bonhoeffer accepted much of the critical scholarship of his day; we have student notes which attest to this fact. In his early lectures he spoke of the Genesis account of Creation as a legend. Yet, he could also proclaim "the word of God is neither fiction nor fairy tale nor myth; on the contrary one must read it word for word like a child and learn to rethink completely what the historical critical commentaries teach us."[48] We must never forget that Bonhoeffer was finding his way out of the limitations of his theologically liberal education. Bonhoeffer sought to listen for what the Word of God had to say for his time and his context, even if he did not understand every word. He was willing to make the momentary "intellectual sacrifice" so that he could hear and proclaim the Divine Word:

> Every other place outside the Bible has become too uncertain for me; I am afraid that I will encounter only a divine double of my own self in it. Is it possible, then, for you to comprehend that I would rather make a *sacrificium intellectus* by confessing that I do not yet understand this or that passage in Scripture, with the certainty that it too will one day reveal itself as God's own word. I would rather do that, than on the basis of my own opinion declare: this is what is divine in it and that is what is human (I make the *sacrificium intellectus* in just these matters and only in these matters, that is, with the true God in view! Who after all would not make a *sacrificium intellectus* anywhere in this respect?).[49]

And as is always the case for Bonhoeffer, Jesus Christ is the Divine Word: "Christians live entirely by the truth of God's Word in Jesus Christ."[50] About this he had no doubts.

Bonhoeffer chose to take his stand on the Divine Word, not only because he mistrusted his and every other human word, but because the Word of God contained the only power to change the world around him and within him. "The place where the Bible begins is the one where our own most impassioned ways of thinking break, are thrown back upon themselves, and lose their strength in spray and foam."[51]

29

WAYFINDING CUES

- Bonhoeffer strongly encourages us to read the Bible "against" ourselves—our self-centeredness; not using Scripture to justify our sinful actions, but allowing it to convict us of our sin. Bonhoeffer's life proves that when read in this way, the Bible can be doubly liberating.

- Bonhoeffer encountered the Word of God in a fresh way during his year of study in the United States. Stepping out of his own German Lutheran tradition, he experienced the Christian life in a new way by attending the African American Abyssinian Church and befriending Frank Fisher and the French pacifist, Jean Lasserre. These encounters deepened his view of Scripture and challenged him to reread the Sermon on the Mount as a way of life and not just a theological text. This transformed his whole Christian life and, unbeknownst to him, prepared him for the Nazi period.

- Pastor-scholar is a modern term for a pastor who writes thought-provoking literature on the Christian life. Dietrich Bonhoeffer is a great example of someone who started as a scholar, discovered his calling as a pastor, and revealed himself as a pastor-scholar who wrote heart-moving books like *The Cost of Discipleship* and *Life Together*. We need pastor-scholars in our local churches.

- Bonhoeffer exhorts the church to read, study, and live out the words of the Bible. We must practice the Scriptures by living them.

WAYFINDING QUESTIONS

1. Do you resonate with Bonhoeffer's journey with the Bible? Has there been a period, or defining moment, during which the Bible "ripened" into the Word of God for you?

2. Bonhoeffer describes repentance in a sermon he gave in 1933 that highlights the very personal battle he had with his own self-promoting ego. What does repentance mean? Where in the Bible do you find help in understanding the meaning of repentance?

3. How would you describe your current interaction with the Bible? Are you engaged in Bonhoeffer's trifecta of practice: reading, studying, and living out God's Word?

4. Bonhoeffer believes we should approach the Bible differently than other books—that when we read the Bible we should ask God questions because it is through the Bible that God speaks to us. Can you share an example when God spoke to you through the Bible, or the sort of questions you ask when you read the Bible?

5. Bonhoeffer says we each need a "brother [or sister] as a bearer and proclaimer of the divine word." Are you engaged in giving and receiving this divine word with a brother or sister? What does it look like when we practice doing this? "The Christ in his own heart is weaker than the Christ in the word of his brother; his own heart is uncertain, his brother's is sure."

DEEP WAYFINDING

1. How does a thorough understanding of the Bible help us recognize false ideologies? Can you provide a personal example?

2. Corporately, how do we—as the church—misuse the Bible to justify our actions or inactions?

3. Have you ever used the Bible for your own self-centered purposes?

3

Paths of Discernment
in the Wilderness

WHERE IS GOD FOR ME?

IN THE SUMMER OF 1939, Dietrich Bonhoeffer, the Lutheran pastor and sober-minded leader of the resistance wing of the Confessing Church, was at a crossroads. He had just received his draft notice, obligating him to report for a physical no later than May 22, 1939. Not unlike the first Christians in the early church, who refused to join the military since it required a soldier to pay obeisance to the army's god of protection, Bonhoeffer could not recite the military oath and swear total allegiance to Adolf Hitler, the German "strong man" and acclaimed savior of the German people:

> I swear by God this holy oath, that I will render to Adolf Hitler, Führer of the German Reich and People, Supreme Commander of the Armed Forces, unconditional obedience, and that I am ready, as a brave soldier, to risk my life at any time for this oath.[52]

Knowing his call-up was imminent, Bonhoeffer began devising an escape plan to the United States. Through his contacts at Union Seminary in New York City, where he had studied during the 1930–31 academic year, he sought to create a new life for himself in America. In Germany, the Nazi regime had prohibited his every activity. No longer could he teach, preach, publish, or even enter Berlin, except to visit his parents. The experimental seminary he directed at Finkenwalde had also been shuttered. By 1939, Bonhoeffer lived a kind of "social death" in Germany. In contrast, his American friends, professor Reinhold Niebuhr, his colleague Paul Lehmann, and Union Seminary president Dr. Henry Sloane Coffin, went to work helping Bonhoeffer recapture the life denied him in Germany. Everything refused him in Nazi Germany would be restored to him in America. He could regain his life and sidestep swearing an oath to Adolf Hitler.

Encouraged by his Confessing Christian brothers to go to America, Bonhoeffer used family connections to receive a one-year military deferment. Freedom waited for him on the other side of the Atlantic, just a boat ride away. On June 4, 1939, he set sail on the Bremen, leaving behind his circumscribed existence in the Third Reich. Yet, Bonhoeffer did not experience the emotional release he anticipated on his departure. Instead, the next few weeks were filled with anxiety and indecision, something uncommon to the usually decisive Bonhoeffer. The path before him was clear: stay in repressive Germany or head to freedom in America. But there was more to it than that. What of his obligations and responsibilities as a Christian brother, as a pastor, as a German to those he left behind in Germany, not to mention his immediate family? Suspended on the horns of dilemma, he desperately needed a clear sign from God.

Before departing from Germany, Ruth von Kleist-Retzow, a key supporter of the Finkenwalde Seminary, spoke a blessing over Dietrich, which summed up his situation well:

> God's blessing accompany you from morning till evening, and may what you do for God be returned to you. Someday too all our "whys" will be resolved.[53]

For the faithful Christians in Germany, there were many unanswered "whys" about the monumental changes occurring under Adolf Hitler, but even more so now for the beleaguered Dietrich Bonhoeffer, who carried the extra weight of wondering if he was making the correct decision in leaving Germany and heading to the United States.

Armed with only his Bible and the *Moravian Daily Text*, a devotional book he had been reading since his youth, he longed for clear direction from God. As a part of his urgent desire to hear God's will, he kept a journal during this momentous time in his life, disclosing unusual insight into his immediate thought and spiritual life. On day one of his crossing of the Atlantic Ocean, the *Daily Text* directed him to Isaiah 41:9. Here, in this passage, he received encouragement:

> I took you from the ends of the earth, from its farthest corners I called you. I said, "You are my servant"; I have chosen you and have not rejected you.[54]

He wrote this reflection in his journal revealing the inner battle raging within him, struggling to convince himself of the rightness of his choice in leaving Germany:

> Whether you work over there [Germany] or I work in America, we are both only where God is. God takes us along. Or have I indeed evaded the place where God is? Where is God for me? No, God says: "You are my servant."[55]

Two days later, on June 11, we find Bonhoeffer reflecting on Scripture again. This time wrestling with the reality of his limited perspective as he pondered 1 Corinthians 13:12, "For now we see only a reflection as in a mirror; then we shall see face to face. Now I know in part; then I shall know fully, even as I am fully known." Yet, he maintained his confidence in the centrality of Jesus Christ for his Christian faith:

> If only the doubts about my own path were overcome . . .
> when the confusion of reproaches and excuses, of wishes
> and fears makes everything in us opaque, God sees in all

clarity right through to the bottom. There, however, God finds the very name that he himself has inscribed: Jesus Christ. And thus we will someday see in all clarity right through to the bottom of the divine heart, and there will be one name to read, no, to see there: Jesus Christ.[56]

CONNECTICUT SUMMER HOME

During his stay in America, Union Seminary president Henry Sloane Coffin invited Bonhoeffer to his Connecticut summer home. After the long sea voyage, this respite gave Bonhoeffer the needed time to pray, think, and talk things over with his colleagues and friends. Nestled away in the mountains, the Coffin summer residence also gave him the opportunity to hike in the beautiful Connecticut countryside. Bonhoeffer rhapsodized over the cool and lush vegetation and experienced for the first time the pageantry of fireflies lighting up the early evening darkness, something he had never seen in Germany.

Meals served on the home's veranda gave way to the sort of academic banter that must have been stimulating after the years of unrelenting governmental pressure in his homeland. He and President Coffin discussed the need for more gospel-centered preaching, Coffin describing—in what must have been a humorous exchange—the preaching of Union professor of ethics Reinhold Niebuhr as "a half hour about the 'failures of man' and the last two minutes about the 'grace of God.'"[57] This sort of churchman shop talk surely stirred longings in Bonhoeffer for the opportunity to return to this way of life. Indeed, America offered Bonhoeffer not only security from the Gestapo, but an opportunity to return to the academic life of foregone years. The temptation must have been overwhelming. His friend professor Paul Lehmann had worked hard to set up teaching, preaching, and other academic work during his stay, which his American hosts believed would be for two years, if not longer.

But there was more. Bonhoeffer also mentions the great love and care the Coffin family showered on him, taking time to kneel in prayer with him around the breakfast table—beseeching the Lord on behalf of Bonhoeffer's Christian brothers in Germany—an experience which "almost overwhelmed" him.[58]

His journal entry on Thursday, June 15, 1939 mentions one more interesting tidbit about a drive into the countryside to meet up with a woman acquaintance. Who she is, he does not mention. But their conversation intimates that it was a woman to whom he was close. They took time to discuss whether a good musical education was possible in New York. Was she, like Bonhoeffer, a gifted musician? They also spoke about raising children, an odd thing to discuss among casual male-female relationships.[59] No, everything we know leads us to believe that she was more than a passing acquaintance, quite possibly someone for whom Bonhoeffer had romantic feelings. If this supposition is correct, Bonhoeffer may have had an additional reason to stay in America: companionship. Whatever the case may be, his relationship with this woman did not settle the overriding question in his mind of whether to stay in America or return to Germany, though some clarity was forming. He wrote a letter to one of his contacts in America, Henry Leiper, stating he would be returning to Germany no later than one year from now.

There were many good reasons to remain in America: a chance to teach again, preach, publish, not to mention the security that a life in the States would bring. As tempting as these opportunities were, they were all one thicket blocking Bonhoeffer's vision of the path he needed to escape the wilderness of doubt. For Bonhoeffer, the way forward lay off the beaten path and into unfamiliar terrain of the kingdom.

NEW YORK CITY

Bonhoeffer returned to New York City on June 16. The World's Fair was in progress that summer in the city. He was turned off by the "Temple of Religion" at the fair, calling the building it was housed in, an old movie theatre, "dreadful."[60] That Sunday he attended Riverside Church, a bastion of early twentieth-century theological liberalism. His critique was severe. He noted sarcastically that the text used for the sermon was from James, not the biblical book, but probably William James, an American philosopher of religion. His words have a force of disdain that must be read to appreciate:

> . . . the whole thing a discreet, opulent, self-satisfied cel-
> ebration of religion. With such an idolization of religion,
> the flesh, which was accustomed to being held in check
> by the word of God, revives. Such preaching renders
> people libertines, egoistic, indifferent.[61]

Undeterred, he attended another service later that day seeking the spiritual nourishment the lonely Bonhoeffer needed: praying together, singing together, listening together. This time he received just what he needed at Broadway Presbyterian Church, a church on the conservative side of the Fundamentalist/Modernist divide in America at the time:

> The sermon was astounding, about "our likeness with
> Christ." A completely biblical sermon—particularly
> good the sections: "we are blameless like Christ," "we
> are tempted like Christ!" Later this will eventually be a
> center of resistance long after Riverside Church will have
> become a temple of idolatry.[62]

But it was not simply the bibliocentric contrast between the liberal Riverside Church and the conservative Broadway Presbyterian that caught Bonhoeffer's attention. He took notes on the latter's sermon because it addressed his own plight. Bonhoeffer wrote: "Let us never pity ourselves; let us never be tragic. There is nothing tragic about suffering. Let us realize that through suffering God is conforming us to his likeness, that our suffering is only part of God's suffering and that finally victory and triumph is his." So, a life of suffering, he concluded, "is the root of victorious living."[63]

Bonhoeffer knew about what he wrote. In Germany, he had experienced genuine persecution. His life had been severely lim-ited because he would not bend the knee to Nazi ideology. Yet, his first few days in America revealed a different sort of suffer-ing, an existential dread settling upon him as he wrestled with the implications of staying in America. He began to contemplate returning to Germany, sooner rather than later, but that would surely entail imprisonment, or worse, since he was determined not to swear a solemn oath to Adolf Hitler. He did not know yet how to cut the Gordian knot of living in Nazi Germany as a Christian, even as he continued to be on the lookout for the right sword.

Events moved fast for Bonhoeffer during these trying weeks. Two days later, on June 20, he visited with Henry Leiper and let him know that he was turning down the offer to take care of German refugees. Bonhoeffer experienced the first of what would be many negative reactions as he declined the opportunities that Leiper, Coffin, Niebuhr, and Lehmann had worked so hard to attain for him. "He was visibly disappointed and indeed somewhat put out," Bonhoeffer recorded matter-of-factly in his journal.[64]

Even with Leiper's disappointment, it felt good to make a decision, even a small one, after so many days of indecision. This decision did not settle the big question about returning to Germany that loomed ever larger in his mind, however:

> The reasons that one puts forward to others and oneself
> for an action are certainly not sufficient. One can simply
> give reasons for anything. In the end one acts out of a
> level that remains hidden from us. Because of that one
> can only pray that God will wish to judge us and forgive
> us. And more, at the end of the day, I can only pray that
> God may hold merciful judgment over this day and all
> decisions. It is now in God's hands.[65]

The uncertainty did not relent, but continued through Wednesday, June 21 into Thursday, June 22. The *Moravian Daily Text* provided a scriptural quote from Malachi 3:3 that elucidated his inner situation perfectly: "God will sit as a refiner and purifier of silver." This elicited a reaction from Bonhoeffer that shows him beginning to believe God was speaking to him through its pages, "Once again the *Daily Text* speaks so harshly . . ."[66] His angst was compounded by the fear that war might start in Europe before he returned, shutting him out of his homeland and ending all possibility of pastoring his brothers and family through the conflict. The accumulative effect of this period of intense anguish and uncertainty led him to move his return date up to August 12. This time of hypersensitivity to the plight of the Confessing Church and the Jews in Germany made him alert to the less virulent but growing anti-Semitism in America, noting in his journal an advertisement for a mountain resort which read, "1,000 feet—too high for Jews," and "Gentiles preferred."[67]

BREAKTHROUGH

The long-sought breakthrough he was searching for finally arrived on Monday, June 26:

> Today I happened to read from 2 Timothy 4:21 "come before the winter"—Paul's plea to Timothy. Timothy is to share the suffering of the apostle and not be ashamed. "Come before the winter"—otherwise it might be too late. That is haunting me the whole day.[68]

The conviction was strong upon him that this verse was for this moment. After weeks of seeking God's will, he was confident this verse was for him. Bonhoeffer the theologian only paused momentarily to evaluate the correctness of using Scripture in such an uncontextualized way. But the conviction this was from God was so strong he simply moved on to the conclusion, "'Come before the winter.'—it is not a misuse of the Scripture if I allow this to be said of me. If God gives me the grace for that."[69] This conviction from God only accelerated his desire to return to Germany at once.

The out-loud rumblings in Bonhoeffer's soul had made their way to his friend Paul Lehmann, causing Paul to write a letter to Dietrich beseeching him to stay. Lehmann noted how helpful Bonhoeffer's contribution to the theological discussion in America would be, summarizing it as a "theological hour of destiny."[70] He pursued this line of reasoning arguing that Bonhoeffer's responsibility to American theological students was ever as much as his responsibility to his German students. In fact more, because American students needed the "cross fertilization with the European continental theological tradition."[71] Therefore, it was "unthinkable" that he should return to Germany so soon.[72]

Lehmann's argument proved insufficient. The heartfelt plea from his dear friend was outmatched by Bonhoeffer's fervent desire and godly conviction to depart from America as soon as possible. When he learned that his brother Karl Friedrich booked a ticket to leave on the eighth of July, he immediately moved his departure date up. Paul would not be so easily dissuaded, traveling all the way from Columbus, Ohio to plead his case for Dietrich to stay in America. Even up to the day before his departure, Bonhoeffer reveals in his journal, "Paul is still trying to keep me here."[73] Bonhoeffer asked his friend's forgiveness for all the trouble he had put him through but made it clear that it was "no longer possible" for him to stay in America.[74] "The journey is over," he wrote with finality.[75] Even though Lehmann remained disappointed with his friend, his disappointment did nothing to lessen his admiration for Bonhoeffer. Lehmann wrote his father, Timothy Lehmann, president of Elmhurst College, a week after Bonhoeffer's departure about his impression of Bonhoeffer in 1939. One senses in his words not only the loss of friendship, but also of what might have been if Bonhoeffer had stayed and theologically engaged the American church:

> The outstanding impression one gets from being with him and from hearing his account of the work he is doing is that the only power for living in a complex broken world is the Christian gospel. Here is a man and a group who are so completely committed to Christ in life that it has become axiomatic to them that they may have to die for Him. And they are ready. . . . When the New Testament talks about one's "joy being full" it lays down what these men are experiencing now . . . The German Confessional Church is re-enacting the book of Acts. Therein is its power, therein is the hope for the only possible German future.[76]

ON HIS WAY HOME

As for Bonhoeffer, now that he was aboard the ship and heading home, he could reflect more positively on his brief time in America, "I am glad that I was there, and glad that I am on my way home again. I have perhaps learned more in this month than in the entire year nine years ago; at least I have come to realize important things for all future personal decisions," and, "since I have been aboard the ship, the internal tension about the future has stopped. I can think about the abbreviated time in America without reproach."[77] As an added explanation point to his twenty-six days in America, the *Daily Text* provided a reading from Psalm 119:73, "It is good for me that I was humbled, so that I might learn your statutes."

His time in the wilderness of America clarified his mission in Germany, providing him perspective from a distance, to see the path pointing forward that he must follow. The road before him called for great courage and a willingness to sacrifice, even his life if called for—though Bonhoeffer had no desire to be a martyr. He could not fulfill his calling in Germany by sitting out the war in security in America. And so his return to Germany and subsequent work as a double agent for the German resistance was the culmination of a clarifying thought he first wrote in a letter to his Union professor Reinhold Niebuhr, while still at Dr. Coffin's summer home:

> I must live through this difficult period of our national history with the Christian people of Germany. I will have no right to participate in the reconstruction of Christian life in Germany after the war if I do not share the trials of this time with my people . . . Christians in Germany will face the terrible alternative of either willing the defeat of their nation in order that Christian civilization may survive, or willing the victory of their nation and thereby destroying our civilization. I know which of these alternatives I must choose; but I cannot make that choice in security.[78]

WAYFINDING CUES

- Bonhoeffer's struggle to hear the will of God in 1939 offers us a very good example on how to seek God's direction: He read the Bible closely, followed a daily rule of life with the *Moravian Text*, kept a journal, talked openly with trusted Christian friends, and prayed daily.

- Bonhoeffer received the impression God was providing him direction when he read 2 Timothy 4:21. In this passage Paul asks Timothy to come to him before winter. Bonhoeffer took an honest, visceral question to the text and understood this Bible passage as God's leading him to return to Germany before war broke out.

- Peace was the fruit of his following the will of God, even in hard decisions and hard times.

WAYFINDING QUESTIONS

1. What do you think about Bonhoeffer's personal interaction with Scripture? His use of the *Moravian Daily Text* as a devotional book? Describe how the reading of the Bible helps you make better decisions during trying times.

2. Can you list the main reasons for Bonhoeffer to stay in America? Would you describe these as temptations or opportunities?

3. Why does Bonhoeffer have such a negative reaction to the sermon at Riverside Church? How did this sermon differ from the one given by Dr. John H. McComb at Broadway?

4. Bonhoeffer believes that a specific Bible verse, 2 Timothy 4:21, is meant for him at this moment. Do you think this is an appropriate way to read the Bible? Has the Bible ever spoken to you in this way?

5. Describe the internal peace Bonhoeffer experienced once he was on his way to Germany. Why was this the right decision for him?

DEEP WAYFINDING

1. How do you discern the will of God in your life, especially during the most difficult times?

2. How is it possible that Bonhoeffer and his Confessing brothers were experiencing a "joy being full" in the midst of Nazi oppression of the church?

4

Paths to Conspiracy

WITH HIS TIME IN the American wilderness behind him, Bonhoeffer took the decisive step in 1939 to join the conspiracy against Adolf Hitler.

Bonhoeffer's brother-in-law Hans von Dohnányi, a lawyer working in the Germany military intelligence (*Abwehr*), had been recruiting him hard for some time. The *Abwehr* contained a cell of anti-Nazi resisters intent on removing Adolf Hitler from power. The extraordinariness of the moment was not lost on Bonhoeffer. This was especially true for one who had been working so long for peaceable regime change in Germany. He ruminated on his situation in Germany, "one may ask whether there have ever before in human history been people with so little ground under their feet—people to whom every available alternative seemed equally intolerable, repugnant, and futile."[79]

As early as 1933, shortly after Hitler had been installed as chancellor of Germany, Bonhoeffer authored an essay entitled, "The Church and the Jewish Question." In this prescient writing, Bonhoeffer revealed his prophetic insight, calling the church to consider its response towards a government acting illegitimately. Since Lutheranism taught a two-sphere theology, where the church and state should not mettle in the other's jurisdiction, his essay was pushing the church uncomfortably towards action outside its traditional boundaries. He wrote:

> There are thus three possibilities for action that the church can take vis-a-vis the state: first, (as we have said), questioning the state as to the legitimate state character of its actions, that is, making the state responsible for what it does. Second is service to the victims of the state's actions . . . The third possibility is not just to bind up the wounds of the victims beneath the wheel but to seize the wheel itself. Such an action would be direct political action on the part of the church. This is only possible and called for if the church sees the state to be failing in its function of creating law and order, that is, if the church perceives that the state, without any scruples, has created either too much or too little law and order . . . There would be too little if any one group of citizens is deprived of its rights. There would be too much in the case of an attack, coming from the state, on the nature of the church and its proclamation, such as obligatory exclusion of baptized Jews from the Church.[80]

His assessment of the role of the church in state and social matters did not remain theoretical for long. He soon called for action. It is important to recognize that Bonhoeffer believed there was a necessary path of nonviolent resistance before he even considered entering a conspiracy to remove Adolf Hitler from power. As late as the mid-1930s he was still advocating for a peaceful approach, arguing in the *The Cost of Discipleship*:

> By refusing to pay back the enemy in his own coin, and by preferring to suffer without [violent] resistance, the Christian exhibits the sinfulness of contumely and insult . . . [because]the shameful assault, the deed of violence and the act of exploitation are still evil. The disciple must realize this, and bear witness to it as Jesus did, *just because this is the only way evil can be met and overcome*"[81] (emphasis added).

Larry Rasmussen, in his book *Dietrich Bonhoeffer—His Significance for North America*, traces the five steps Bonhoeffer took before he entered the conspiratorial work within the *Abwehr*.

Step One: Unambiguous evidence must be available of gross misrule by the government. Bonhoeffer possessed intimate knowledge of extra-legal Nazi overreach. His immediate family and their spouses held key positions within the government, which gave him access to this sort of sensitive information.

Step Two: He must wait for those who are in higher positions (political/military) to act and fail. By 1940, Hitler's military and economic success exceeded all expectations, convincing top political and military leaders to postpone action against the Fuehrer. The same top leaders had squandered more favorable opportunities during the early part of Hitler's rule.

Step Three: One must exhaust all nonviolent action and legal means before pursuing violent resistance. Bonhoeffer tried unsuccessfully to move the church towards nonviolent, political action. The church rebuffed his attempts as too radical at every turn.

Step Four: Only the necessary minimal use of force must be employed. Through his ecumenical contacts, Bonhoeffer floated the idea of arresting Hitler and calling an immediate cease-fire with the allies. The allies remained skeptical the *coup d'état* could be successful. Finally, they demanded nothing short of unconditional surrender on the part of Germany. This left the conspirators with no other plan of action than to assassinate Hitler.

Step Five: Assurance that action will be successful in creating the necessary political leadership to rule afterwards. The conspirators had a few key generals who were ready to assume control of the country once Hitler was dead. As it turned out, the preparation for the time after Hitler proved unnecessary. The several attempts made on Hitler's life were unsuccessful, including two attempts by Bonhoeffer's group of conspirators.[82]

ETHICAL CONSIDERATIONS

Per usual with Bonhoeffer, his move into the world of the conspiracy was more than simple political theater. He believed the events consuming Germany were spiritual in nature: "How can one close one's eyes at the fact that the demons themselves have taken over rule of the world, that it is the powers of darkness who had made an awful conspiracy."[83]

He set himself upon the task to try to understand the spiritual element swaying the German nation. His years of biblical study gave him the right interpretative tools to discern the true nature of Hitler's rule. When Hitler referred to the German nation as the "volk," or folkish state, the German leader rummaged back into Germany's pre-Christian, pagan past for a deeper meaning of the concept. According to the American war correspondent William Shirer and author of the monumental *The Rise and Fall of the Third Reich*, Hitler's use of *volk* connoted a "primitive, tribal community based on blood and soil."[84] Hitler did not envision Germany as a collection of individuals, but always as a collective community. He saw an ancient spiritual community pregnant with meaning and historical purpose, not a defeated community, devastated by circumstances beyond its control, stemming from the First World War.

Hitler called the German people to this primal vision of community. He lashed them with his words to rise up under his leadership, the "great leader" (*Der Fuehrer*) whom Providence had selected, and to reverse the injustices of the Versailles Treaty. This Germanic pagan vision of revenge and conquest under the divinely appointed strong man, and the restoration of greatness of the German *volk*, resonated with many Germans in the early twentieth century.

But even more grave, Bonhoeffer's study of the church made it possible for him to recognize the reasons for the messianic hold Hitler had over Germany. Hitler placed himself in relation to Germany in a way which, though diabolical, was not dissimilar to the relationship between Jesus and the church. Just as Jesus was the embodiment of the church, Hitler sought to be the living embodiment of the German *volk*. The ultimate end of this was not only that Hitler became the spokesperson for the German community, but rather the apotheosis of Adolf Hitler. Hitler positioned himself to be the hope and salvation of Germany.

Dr. Hans Kerrl, Hitler's minister for church affairs, expressed this sentiment without equivocation in 1935, stating that Christianity does not consist "in faith in Christ as the Son of God. That makes me laugh . . . No, True Christianity is not dependent upon the Apostles' Creed . . . True Christianity is represented by the party, and the German people are now called by the party and especially by the Fuehrer to a real Christianity . . . The Fuehrer is the herald of a new revelation."[85]

BONHOEFFER LEAVES THE CONFESSING CHURCH AND JOINS THE CONSPIRACY

In Bonhoeffer's judgment, the night of November 9, 1938, ended any sort of legitimate claim the Confessing Church had as an oppositional force to the Nazi government in Germany. The Nazis dubbed it "Crystal Night," as they terrorized the Jews, smashing their shops, burning their synagogues, and beating them as police officers sat idly by watching. The Confessing Church remained silent the next day and the days following "Crystal Night."

Bonhoeffer underlined in his Bible two verses from Psalm 74: "They are burning all the houses of God in the land," and "No prophet speaks any longer." He put the date of "Crystal Night" beside the two verses.

The Berlin church historian Karl Kupisch summarized the Confessing Church's position well when he wrote, "the Confessing Church was in no way opposed to government policy but primarily and exclusively opposed to the heresies and violent measures of the 'German Christians' within the church. Had Hitler only left the church in peace . . . the Confessing Church would never have come into existence."[86]

Bonhoeffer had seen enough and effectively withdrew from any further participation within the Confessing Church. His final word on the passive role the church played took the shape of a confession to the world. He wrote, the church "was silent when she should have cried out because the blood of the innocent was crying aloud to heaven . . . the church confesses that she has witnessed the lawless application of brutal force, the physical and spiritual suffering of countless innocent, oppression, hatred and murder, and that she has not raised her voice on behalf of the victims."[87]

This was one key reason Bonhoeffer joined the conspiratorial group within German Military Intelligence when he returned to Germany in 1939. They were willing to take action against Hitler when the church was not. For his part, because of his international connections, Bonhoeffer held exciting potential for the work of the conspiracy. Reaching out to church colleagues in Sweden, Switzerland, and England, he put forward a twofold message: first, the church is doomed if the Nazis conquer Europe, and second, there is an anti-Nazi resistance plan to assassinate Adolf Hitler, set up a temporary government, and end the war.

In a letter to Anglican Bishop George Bell in England, a longtime friend of Bonhoeffer's and a member of the House of Lords, Bonhoeffer stated the current situation in unadulterated and realistic terms: "The question at stake in the German Church is no longer an internal issue, but it is the question of the existence of Christianity in Europe."[88]

This comment added the necessary motivation, if any was needed, for church leaders to work closely with Bonhoeffer to advance the cause of the German conspiracy within the British government. This was uphill work from the beginning since prime minister Winston Churchill had serious doubts about the viability of a substantial resistance movement in Nazi Germany and foreign secretary Anthony Eden did not care for Bishop Bell, referring to him as "this pestilent priest."[89] There was something to be said for Churchill's skepticism. In the *Abwehr*, one of the key centers of opposition to the Nazis, there were at most fifty people committed to the resistance out of total of thirteen thousand working in the organization.

Hans Von Dohnányi saw the value in Bonhoeffer's ecumenical connections. Desperate to inform the allies of the state of the resistance, there were few avenues to do this, and even fewer political leaders who took them seriously. Yet there was a story to be told in this "war behind the war." Von Dohnányi had been documenting the illegalities and atrocities of the Nazi regime from 1933 onward.[90] His wife called the work of documenting his "private practice," while he referred to the document as his "portfolio of curiosities" or at other times, the "scandal chronicle."[91] Von Dohnányi's unique vantage point within military intelligence gave him personal entry to high Nazi leaders such as Goebbels, Goring, Himmler, and even Hitler, as well as access to sensitive plans outlining coercive orders and acts of terror. He even obtained film evidence of the atrocities committed by the SS in Poland. His hope of sharing this information with allied governments rested in no small part on Bonhoeffer's unique set of foreign friends and colleagues.

Bonhoeffer did his part. Meeting George Bell, bishop of Chichester, in Sweden he handed over the names of well-positioned conspirators ready to govern after Hitler's death. Bonhoeffer spoke for his fellow conspirators when he told his foreign colleagues, "I pray for the defeat of my country, for I believe that this is the only way it can pay for the suffering which it has caused the world."[92]

Actively working against Germany was no easy task for the generals and officers whom Bonhoeffer worked alongside in the *Abwehr*. Everyone wrestled with the guilt of betraying their country. Bonhoeffer found here a unique setting to use his pastoral skills. Bonhoeffer's friend Eberhard Bethge wrote about one such story of a German officer who had experienced the Nazi atrocities in Poland firsthand. He sought out Bonhoeffer's counsel on his role as a German officer in the conspiracy. Bonhoeffer assured him, "'Treason' had become true patriotism, and what was normally 'patriotism' had become treason."[93] Bonhoeffer also tried to salve his brother-in-law's conscience without compromising his biblical ethical view of killing, "murder is still murder, even when, as in the case of Hitler, it is absolutely necessary. One must be prepared to take the guilt for this sin upon oneself."[94] Bonhoeffer added that if he could get near enough to Hitler, he would throw the bomb himself.

As a pastor, the counsel he gave the conspirators was not easy. It caused him to question his core identity as a Christian minister. Had his actions disqualified him from his pastoral office? Could he continue to serve the Lord's Supper? These became persistent, nagging questions in his life.

OPERATION 7

One positive result of all his travels abroad was the building of a network of individuals who he could count on to help when asked. There was at least one instance when his connections allowed Bonhoeffer to help facilitate the escape of Jews out of Germany. Known as Operation 7, this escape plan was instigated out of the offices of the *Abwehr*. What started as a plan to help seven Jews flee to safety quickly became fourteen. Bonhoeffer used his relationships with the Swiss theologian Karl Barth and the president of the Switzerland Federation to acquire the necessary entry visas. One of the fourteen was Charlotte Friedenthal, a Jewish Christian who worked on staff within the Confessing Church.

All his inner questions and wrestling of conscience came to an end when he and Hans, and Han's wife and Bonhoeffer's sister, Christine, were arrested on April 5, 1943. Bonhoeffer spent a good part of his time in prison fending off interrogations attempting to unravel the network of conspiratorial actors. When they questioned how a pastor from the Confessing Church could be of any value working for the war effort, he cleverly replied, "Military Intelligence works with anyone, with communists and with Jews, so why not also with Confessing Church people?"[95]

Bonhoeffer was steadfast in not revealing any names or information that might compromise someone or undermine the plans of the conspiracy. By this time his mission had become simple and clear. After the war Bishop Bell offered an insightful epitaph on Bonhoeffer's work against the Nazis, "He was quite clear in his convictions, and for all that he was so young and unassuming, he saw the truth and spoke it out with absolute freedom and without fear."[96]

"MURDER IS STILL MURDER": A BRIEF EXCURSUS ON BONHOEFFER'S ETHICAL VIEW OF KILLING HITLER

Though Bonhoeffer plunged into the shadowy world of the conspiracy to eliminate Adolf Hitler, he didn't completely detach himself from his role as a Christian theologian. He continued to think through the implications of committing an assassination. From his ethical perspective, to assassinate someone, even Hitler, was still a breaking of God's sixth commandment. He could not easily justify killing of any kind. It was a sin to kill another human being. Even protecting your neighbor, even your nearest neighbor, did not override the biblical commandment to not murder. The sixth commandment was absolute in Bonhoeffer's eyes.

Yet, as Christians, God called us to love our neighbor as ourselves, Bonhoeffer reckoned. Did not the Lord Jesus reduce the entire law down to two commandments? "Love the Lord your God with all your heart and with all your soul and with all your mind and with all your strength. The second is this: Love your neighbor as yourself" (Mark 12:30–31). What did this mean in this time of Nazi control and persecution, filled with the violence of war and death camps? Bonhoeffer believed it created a responsibility for the Christian towards protecting one's neighbor—a responsibility towards action, including the action to kill Adolf Hitler.

So, there was an ethical tension between the commandment not to kill and the commandment to love your neighbor as yourself. Bonhoeffer refused to resolve the ethical tension. If you murder, you sin. Still, you are responsible to love your neighbor. These were indeed extraordinary times where all traditional ethical frameworks faltered.

Bonhoeffer was not just playing theological games. There was wisdom built into the tension. Justifying murder based on loving your neighbor might open a flood gate for easy killing. The Christian needed to wrestle with the ethical dilemma, he reasoned. And beyond that, the Christian must recognize the blood on their hands and the need for repentance and forgiveness. In this act you will have sinned and will need the mercy of God. It was with such ethical reasoning that he helped the military officers and fellow conspirators move forward with their plans to assassinate Hitler.

WAYFINDING CUES

- Bonhoeffer used every available mechanism within the democratic process to try and unseat Adolf Hitler.

- He also urged the church to fend off the Nazi false ideology of racial superiority by holding on tightly to the Bible's teaching that all races are one in Christ.

- He recognized that his time was extraordinary and most times in history are not. We should be careful not to draw too easily on Bonhoeffer's actions as part of a conspiracy, recognizing we do not live in the same extraordinary circumstances in which he did.

- He offered one final wayfinding cue when he joined the conspiracy: he used his best spiritual and theological lights to filter his actions through a biblical lens. In such an extraordinary time when everyone struggled to find biblical ground on which to stand firm, his attempt to do so is still an exemplary wayfinding example for us all.

WAYFINDING QUESTIONS

1. In his essay, "The Church and the Jewish Question," Bonhoeffer writes about the responsibilities of the state. What are the responsibilities of the state towards its citizens? How were the Nazis not living up to these responsibilities?

2. Did Jesus teach a nonviolent approach to life? If so, what are the implications for us today?

3. Was it morally and biblically allowable for Bonhoeffer to participate in the conspiracy? Can a pastor remain in his position if he participates in an assassination attempt?

4. What was so alluring about Hitler's call to enter the primitive German community based on "blood and soil"? What sort of political messages do you find alluring today?

5. What does it mean to say that "Hitler sought to be the living embodiment of the German *volk*"? Is this a form of idolatry?

6. Based on this chapter, why did the Confessing Church struggle to confront Hitler and the Nazi government?

7. What are the strengths of Hans von Dohnányi's approach to undermining the Nazi regime?

DEEP WAYFINDING

1. Could you work against your country if it took a turn away from what you thought was right? How would you judge this turning away?

2. Do you agree or disagree with Bonhoeffer's ethical tension on the assassination of Adolf Hitler? What do you think is the Christian position on this issue?

3. Bonhoeffer lamented the Confessing Church's failures in his written confession on behalf of the church. In what areas today might we, the body of Christ, be too silent or complicit, allowing evil to flourish? What actions could we take to stand against evil?

5

Paths into the Future
of the Church

On April 30, 1944, a little over a year into his imprisonment, Bonhoeffer wrote a letter containing a new line of theological inquiry to his best friend and theological dialogue partner, Eberhard Bethge. These new "theological thoughts," Bonhoeffer confessed, might catch Bethge off guard and "surprise, or perhaps even worry" him.[97] What was so revolutionary about these new ideas that Bonhoeffer felt the need to attach a warning label to them?

His many years of work on behalf of the Confessing Church had opened Bonhoeffer's eyes to a new reality about German culture, indeed in the greater Western world. One of the bedrock assumptions of Western Christianity throughout the ages had been the idea that humanity was *religious a priori*—that is, at their core, people were religious by nature.

What if this assumption was wrong? What if people were essentially nonreligious? What would it mean for the church in the West? It was these set of questions that sent Bonhoeffer exploring a new paradigm for the church:

> We are approaching a completely religionless age; people
> as they are now simply cannot be religious anymore

. . . But our entire nineteen hundred years of Christian preaching and theology are built on the *"religious a priori"* in human beings.[98]

Bonhoeffer suddenly found himself on a journey to discover Christianity after the age of religion. The signs that the age of religion was over, he believed, were all around him:

> The movement toward human autonomy . . . has reached a certain completeness in our age. Human beings have learned to manage all important issues by themselves, without recourse to a "Working hypothesis: God." The world, now that it has become conscious of itself and the laws of its existence, is sure of itself . . . Failures, things going wrong, can't shake the world's confidence in the necessity of its course and its development; such things are accepted with fortitude and sobriety as part of the bargain, and even an event like this war is no exception.[99]

Bonhoeffer surmised that the world had "come of age"—to use his arresting phrase. It had left its infancy and become an adult. And just as an adult relies more and more upon oneself, its need for its parent diminishes. In short, religion no longer was needed in a "world come of age." This insight suggested to Bonhoeffer that religion was not something innate—*religious a priori*—but simply a stage which humanity was passing through.

deus ex machina
"god from the machine"; when a hopeless situation is rescued by an unexpected outside power or event, typically as a plot device in a novel or play.

This new perspective led Bonhoeffer to critique church apologetics based on *religious a priori*. He came to believe the church's approach had become *passe* and now, as a result, misdirected:

> Religious people speak of God at a point where human knowledge is at an end . . . or where human strength fails. Actually, it's a *deus ex machina* that they're always bringing on the scene . . . thus always exploiting human weakness or human limitations. Inevitably that lasts only

until human beings become powerful enough to push the boundaries a bit further and God is no longer needed as *deus ex machina*.[100]

Bonhoeffer chastised the preacher who "set about to drive people to despair, and then they have a game they can win."[101] He referred to this apologetical approach as the "God of the gaps."[102] Christianity is the answer to all questions that are beyond our human understanding—God fills in the gaps of knowledge.

But in an age of unparalleled scientific achievement the gaps were decreasing at an exponential rate. This human achievement served to increase human confidence that just around the corner every question eventually could be answered, every human problem resolved. In effect, the apologetics from the age of religion played into the hands of the strengths of the world. Christian arguments on behalf of the faith had become unconvincing when the intellectual landscape kept shifting in favor of modern man. Bonhoeffer concluded that the church was in retreat with no more ground on which to fall back. And worse yet, it was tragically unaware of this new reality:

> In very different forms the Christian apologetic is now moving against this self-confidence. It is trying to persuade this world that has come of age that it cannot live without "God" as its guardian.[103]

But what about "death" and "guilt"? Bonhoeffer conceded for the moment that Christian apologetics were still getting good mileage out of these two existential questions:

> But what happens if someday they no longer exist as such, or if they are being answered "without God"?[104]

As Bonhoeffer reflected on his moment in history, he recognized that the church had nowhere left to reposition itself, to take a stand, if it continued to believe current apologetics could prevail. He worked to drive home the point that humanity was no longer religious!

RELIGIONLESS CHRISTIANITY IN THE STRENGTHS OF THE WORLD

The question arose, therefore, how the church should reorient its approach for a religionless age. The answer, Bonhoeffer suggested, was not further retreat, but to advance. Christianity must enter into the strengths of the world and claim the world and all its success for Jesus Christ. Here we will discover a new Christianity—shred of its *religious a priori*—a religionless Christianity. Just as the apostle Paul first recognized that circumcision was no longer a requirement for the people of God, Bonhoeffer postulated that religion is no longer necessary for Christianity, if indeed it ever was. "Religious Christianity" searches for the last remaining place of solid ground not occupied by the world come of age; "religionless Christianity" enters into the world, and all its achievements, and claims it all for Christ—the Creator of the world.

Sadly, the cutting short of Bonhoeffer's life did not allow him time to work out all the ways in which a "religionless Christianity" would revitalize the Christian life; this undoubtedly would have been a significant focus of his future work. What he left us, though, is a tantalizing mix of theological and prophetic insights that leave us longing for more. He believed the future of the church would be at least useful, if not quite sanguine, if it would embrace this new reality. Considering he was a condemned man writing from a prison cell as the world was literally falling apart around him, his words provided Bethge a breathtaking eschatological perspective of hope about the future of the church:

> It is not for us to predict the day—but the day will come—when people will once more be called to speak the word of God in such a way that the world is changed and renewed. It will be a new language, perhaps quite nonreligious language, but liberating and redeeming like Jesus's language, so that people will be alarmed and yet overcome by its power—the language of a new righteousness and truth, a language proclaiming that God makes peace with humankind and that God's kingdom is drawing near. "They

shall fear and tremble because of all the good and all the prosperity I provide for them" (Jer. 33:9).[105]

WHERE WILL WE FIND THIS NEW LANGUAGE?

Bonhoeffer spent the better part of his prison sentence reading and rereading the Old Testament. His immersion into the Hebrew Scriptures caused him to question the classical Christian position that life on this earth is secondary to the world beyond. Indeed, his eschatological vision—his understanding of the future—was deeply reshaped from an "otherworldly" to a "this-worldly" perspective: "What matters is not the beyond, but this world, how it is created and preserved, is given laws, reconciled, and renewed."[106] He drilled deeper into this new perspective:

> Redemption now means being redeemed out of sorrows, hardships, anxieties, and longings, out of sin and death, in a better life beyond. But should this really be the essence of the proclamation of Christ in the Gospels and Paul? I dispute this. The Christian hope of resurrection is different from the mythological [misplaced view of eternal life] in that it refers people to their life on earth in a wholly new way, and more sharply than the O.T.[107]

Bonhoeffer came to view the gospel as a continuation and completion of God's desire to see his people flourish on earth—the Old Testament conception of *shalom*. "Never did Jesus question anyone's health and strength or good fortune as such or regard it as rotten fruit; otherwise, why would he have made sick people well or given strength back to the weak? Jesus claims all of human life, in all its manifestations, for himself and for the kingdom of God."[108] It was here, in the midst of the world's achievements and advancements, that he saw an opening to bring the gospel to a world come of age.

Bonhoeffer re-envisioned the world's great leap forward as part of fulfilling the biblical mandate for humanity to create a flourishing world. Human flourishing was not the sin. "One must not find fault with people in their worldliness but rather confront them with God where they are strongest."[109] No, the world come of age missed the mark when it refused to recognize God in the midst of its prosperity. Humanity's newfound self-confidence placed them at the center of the universe and pushed God out of the earthly story. Yet, in Christ, God did not resist: "God consents to be pushed out of the world and onto the cross."[110]

THE CROSS AND CHURCH REFORM

And so having established this new reality of the world, Bonhoeffer returns us to the gospel. It is here that he begins, and sadly only begins, to chart a course forward for the church in a world come of age. It is in the suffering of God on the cross that the church will find a new nonreligious language and life. Historically, the church had held a position of privilege within Western civilization. This is no longer the case. If the church ever returns again to the "center of the village," it will come through humility and powerlessness.[111] If it seeks to bring the gospel into the strengths of the world, it will come through meekness and service. It is with these thoughts in mind that Bonhoeffer offers instruction for church reform in a nonreligious age:

> The church is church only when it is there for others. As a first step it must give away all its property to those in need. The clergy must live solely on the freewill offerings of the congregations and perhaps be engaged in some secular vocation. The church must participate in the worldly tasks of life in community—not dominating but helping and serving. It must tell people in every calling what a life with Christ is, what it means "to be there for others." In particular, our church will have to confront the vices of hubris, the worship of power, envy, and illusionism as the roots of all evil. It will have to speak of moderation, authenticity, trust, faithfulness, steadfastness, patience, discipline, humility, modesty, contentment. It will have to see that it does not underestimate the significance of the human "example" (which has its

origin in the humanity of Jesus and is so important in Paul's writings!).[112]

Before he was arrested, Bonhoeffer was at work on his *Ethics*, what he hoped would be his magnum opus. Here we find him already repositioning the church in a posture of humility, confessing its complicity in the lawlessness of Nazi Germany. "The Church confesses that it has witnessed the lawless application of brutal force, the physical and spiritual suffering of countless innocent people, oppression, hatred, and murder, and that it has not raised its voice on behalf of the victims and has not found ways to hasten to their aid . . . The Church confesses that it has desired security, peace and quiet, possessions and honor, to which it had no right . . ."[113] But confession leads to forgiveness and, ultimately, reconciliation. It is here that Bonhoeffer envisioned the church playing a great role in the necessary healing that must follow the great conflict between nations, and between peoples:

> The "justification and renewal" of the West, therefore, will come only when justice, order, and peace are in one way or another restored, when past guilt is thereby "forgiven," when it is no longer imagined that what has been done can be undone by means of punitive measures and reprisals, and when the church of Jesus Christ, as the fountainhead of all forgiveness, justification, and renewal, is given room to do its work among the nations.[114]

Perhaps beginning with a confession of guilt, the church could be renewed, too, and find the new language it needed to preach to a world come of age. Bonhoeffer ventured to suggest the fiery trial that the church had endured over the past several years might be the refiner's fire needed to speak again with the authority of Jesus Christ:

> There remains an experience of incomparable value. We have for once learned to see the great events of world history from below, from the perspective of the outcast, the suspects, the maltreated, the powerless, the oppressed, the reviled—in short, form the perspective of those who suffer . . . that we should have come to

> look with new eyes at matters great and small, sorrow
> and joy, strength and weakness, that our perception of
> generosity, humanity, justice, and mercy should have
> become clearer, freer, less corruptible.[115]

Paradoxically, then, it is the persecuted church that will find its new voice to speak to a world come of age.

As a prisoner of the Third Reich, Bonhoeffer had all his privileges as a churchman, theologian, and pastor removed from him. Yet it was while stripped of all his former cultural power that he experienced a new spiritual vitality as he interacted with his fellow prisoners and prison guards. It was this new perspective that allowed him to begin to reassess the role of the church in Western society, specifically in a world come of age.

In his "theological thoughts," Bonhoeffer laid out a new prophetic direction for the church that is still well worth contemplating, considering the extent to which the world has become increasingly wide awake to its own strengths in the twenty-first century.

WAYFINDING CUES

- Bonhoeffer recognized that humanity was moving into a new phase, viewing itself as leaving childhood and becoming an adult. As a result, this modern humanity believed it had the capacity to remake the world better, and without God.

- Bonhoeffer also believed that modern man was no longer religious, leaving religion behind as old children's clothes.

- These two insights into the modern self-perception led Bonhoeffer to call for a new apologetic, because the old apologetic—the "God of the gaps," as he called it—no longer worked in the face of the explosion of modern scientific inventions and new ideas about the universe and man.

- Bonhoeffer believed we should meet modern man in his strengths and not seek out his weakness. We should show him that God is not just a thought for the afterworld, but that

God is intensely concerned about humanity during his time on earth. That flourishing, shalom, is a rich part of the salvation message.

- Paradoxically, Bonhoeffer argues, as the world has pushed God out of the world and onto the cross, the church can now begin to see the world from below and serve with humility. The church can no longer proclaim its message from the center of the village, he wrote, but must speak a new language that is as arresting as Jesus' words in the first century. *Ecce homo*—"behold the man," the resurrected Lord—is the new humanity the "world come of age" is searching for.

WAYFINDING QUESTIONS

1. Do you think Bonhoeffer is correct that people are nonreligious by nature? How does your answer to this question shape your gospel interaction with non-Christian Westerners?

2. Do you agree with Bonhoeffer that Christian apologetics relies too much on the "God of the gaps" approach?

3. Bonhoeffer was concerned that the ultimate questions surrounding "death" and "sin" would one day be answered nonreligiously. Has his concern been confirmed in our time?

4. What do you think are some of the "strengths of the world" in the twenty-first century? In your specific city?

5. How do you evaluate Bonhoeffer's call for a more this-worldly theology? Do you think he has interpreted the main message of the Bible correctly in both the Old and New Testaments?

6. Looking back from the twenty-first century, do you think Bonhoeffer's appraisal of a "world come of age" has stood the test of time?

7. What is your response to Bonhoeffer's proposal for church reform in a world come of age?

DEEP WAYFINDING

1. How can you enter into conversation—bring Christ into the strengths of the world—with the successful, the rich, the educated, the creative class, the minimalist, the ecologically conscious, the social activist, or the peacemaker?

2. Do you find that you enter the strengths of the world and applaud or affirm a work which brings human flourishing—making life better for people—and recognize they are doing the "Lord's work"? If so, how might you start with a "yes" to their work and aim to show how their good work is the work God requires of us all? How might this help us invite them into a fuller understanding of God and his great work for the redemption of this world?

3. How have you experienced Bonhoeffer's ideas that confession of guilt and persecution will be gateways to an authentic witness to the world?

6

Paths into South Africa

INTRODUCTION

What does the German Dietrich Bonhoeffer have to say for a troubled church in Africa struggling against the bonds of white supremacy? What does Berlin have to do with Soweto? In this chapter we will consider these questions, emerging with evidence of Bonhoeffer's witness as a wayfinder for the South African church's resistance movement against apartheid. In turn, we can allow the South African church's example to be a wayfinder for us today.

THE CONTEXT OF APARTHEID

The seeds of apartheid were sown with the arrival of the Portuguese explorer Bartolomeu Dias in 1487 at the Cape of Good Hope, paving the way for the settlement of the Dutch East India Company, which established a refreshment colony in 1652 for their journeys to and from India. It was during this first decade that legal status groups were enforced, placing Cape residents in a caste-like system.

Apartheid, as an Afrikaner political program in the twentieth century, was the offspring of a marriage of the Dutch Reformed Church, Afrikaner intelligentsia in the Western Cape, and the inspiration blowing across the Atlantic from America's Jim Crow South. The term (Afrikaans for "apartness") was first used publicly in 1929 by the Rev. J. C. du Plessis, who gave voice to the influential ideas of German missiologist Gustav Warneck. Little did he know how dramatically his ideas of separateness would fund the imagination of future political ideology.

The influential D. F. Malan and his Afrikaner intellectual circle in the Western Cape composed a more extremist plan of separate development. At its heart, apartheid proponents harbored the notion that "separate development" was politically expedient, socially prudent, economically favorable, philosophically justifiable, and biblically warranted. Malan and the National Party gained victory in 1948, and the apartheid system took root. Prime Minister Malan was welcomed with great fanfare in Pretoria on June 1, 1948, where he declared to his Afrikaner base: "In the past, we felt like strangers in our own country, but today South Africa belongs to us once more. For the first time since Union, South Africa is our own. May God grant that it always remains our own."[116]

By the 1970s, the wealthy Afrikaner class had a hegemonic hold on the strings of power in every sector. As inequity grew, the tyranny of apartheid continued to dehumanize and oppress all who were not white Afrikaners. In 1976, the National Party passed the Bantu Education Act, forcing all educators to mediate classroom instruction through the Afrikaans language. This maneuver resulted in a wave of unrest across the country, with the epicenter in Soweto. In the wake of the Soweto Uprising, anti-apartheid leader of the African National Congress Nelson Mandela proclaimed:

> What is now unmistakable, what the current wave of unrest has sharply highlighted, is this: that despite all the window-dressing and smooth talk, apartheid has become intolerable. This awareness reaches over and beyond the particulars of our enslavement. The measure of this truth

is the recognition by our people that under apartheid our lives, individually and collectively, count for nothing.[117]

Sadly, the situation grew more dire through the 1970s and 1980s until the year 1989 when the elections handed power to the National Party's newest leader, F. W. de Klerk, who relented to anti-apartheid pressures and began releasing political prisoners and commencing peace negotiations. The country teetered on the brink of civil war all the way to the finish line on April 27, 1994, when, for the first time in the nation's history, all South Africans marched to the polls and Nelson Mandela was elected the country's first Black president.

BRIDGING CONTEXTS BETWEEN NAZISM AND APARTHEID

Apartheid developed within the ideological structures and powers of Afrikaner civil religion and nationalism. The ideology propagated the notion that Afrikaners held a divine right to the land, as voiced by Prime Minister D. F. Malan, himself a former Dutch Reformed Church minister:

> Our history is the greatest masterpiece of the centuries. We hold this nationhood as our due for it was given us by the Architect of the universe. [God's] aim was the formation of a new nation among the nations of the world . . . The last hundred years have witnessed a miracle behind which must lie a divine plan. Indeed, the history of the Afrikaner reveals a will and a determination which makes one feel that Afrikanerdom is not the work of [human beings] but the creation of God.[118]

In Malan's rhetoric we hear a *volkish* tenor reminiscent of the romantic, nationalist language of Hitler about the preeminent rights of the German *volk*. Comparing and contrasting the suffering of millions of Holocaust victims with the suffering of apartheid's victims can be misguided. However, prominent South African theologian and historian John de Gruchy reminds us that the perspective of the oppressed does not diminish the pain:

> Comparisons between Nazi Germany and Afrikaner-
> dom can be forced, misleading, and wrong in attempting
> to analyze the South African situation, but for those who
> experience the brunt of apartheid, who feel its daily pain,
> the discussion of its relationship to Nazism is academic.
> Dehumanization, discrimination, suffering, poverty, and
> sometimes death in detention is no less real for the vic-
> tims of apartheid than for the victims of any other unjust
> social system.[119]

Bonhoeffer's close friend and ally Eberhard Bethge, who survived
the Nazi terror and greatly involved himself in the South African
church struggle, acknowledged that South Africa was not a to-
talitarian state in the Nazi sense, but he did concede after his 1973
visit to South Africa that it certainly appeared that way to those
who were in the thick of it.

In summary, both the National Socialism of Hitler's Third
Reich and Afrikanerdom's apartheid were oppressive, dehuman-
izing regimes that carried out systemic injustices with varying
degrees of erroneous theological justification, nationalist aspira-
tion, and hegemonic force. Bearing in mind the discontinuities in
the scope of brutality and the incomparable geopolitical scenarios,
the commonalities welcome the reception of Bonhoeffer as a wayfinder for the South African church's struggle.

OFF THE BEATEN PATH WITH CHURCH STRUGGLE LEADERS

It was 1985. Three hundred church leaders from the South African
Council of Churches (SACC), led by General Secretary Beyers
Naudé, marched to Parliament to deliver a petition demanding the
removal of the South African police from Black townships. The
clergy knelt in hymn-singing as the police approached, blasting the
nonviolent protestors with water cannons. The church leaders were
arrested. Three years later, the struggle for liberation was grinding
on. Momentum was growing. The Afrikaner government was digging in their heels. Gathering at St. George's Anglican Cathedral in

Cape Town, prominent leaders from the SACC marched from the refuge of the church's walls to Parliament to protest the banning of Black opposition leaders. The South African police greeted them once again with force in the remaining attempts of the apartheid state to stamp out the fires of nonviolent resistance. The Clerics' March of February 29, 1988 was a pivotal moment for the church struggle. Archbishop Desmond Tutu declared that day that they were choosing to obey God rather than man. Among those involved in the SACC, of interest for our investigation, are several Christian leaders who found inspiration in the witness of Dietrich Bonhoeffer.

That day in 1988 was a culmination of years of confession and resistance to apartheid. No doubt, the holistic assault upon apartheid was a decades-long, multifaceted movement, involving political parties, violent and nonviolent campaigns, student campaigns, the arts, international economic pressures, geopolitical maneuvering amidst the threat of the Soviet Union, and more. Amid these myriad forces collaborating to dethrone injustice, Christian leaders in the South African church played a dynamic and influential role. While there are a host of individuals and ecclesial bodies who were active and consequential dissidents in the decades-long church struggle in South Africa, we will limit our brief investigation here to the witness of four protestant church leaders: Beyers Naudé, Allan Boesak, Manas Buthelezi, and Desmond Tutu.

Naudé, Boesak, Buthelezi, and Tutu were a part of a tapestry of Christian confession and resistance to the apartheid state. Their actions weave in and out of one another's lives, each leaning upon the efforts of another. None stands alone; all stand in solidarity in the struggle to abolish apartheid. Unlike the German context in which Bonhoeffer struggled for the gospel and the soul of the church, these four South African struggle leaders served in different denominations, and their work for liberation spanned decades of dissent. What did these leaders gain from Bonhoeffer's legacy? How was he a wayfinder for them in their own struggle against an evil system?

Among the places where the lives of Naudé, Boesak, Buthelezi, and Tutu intersected, the South African Council of Churches (SACC) is noteworthy. While South Africa never had a "Confessing Church" in the manner of Bonhoeffer's context, the SACC was an ecumenical body that matured in its confession and resistance over the years, beginning in 1968 with the "Message to the People of South Africa," the first public, ecumenical declaration stating the church's belief that apartheid was not just unjust, but a false gospel. In 1973, the SACC convened a conference in Hammanskraal to work out their views on conscientious objection because of the growing violence both within the borders of South Africa and outside where the South African Police and South African Defence Force (SADF) were embroiled in forestalling the threats of anti-apartheid rebel training cells and the guerilla warfare of neighboring Marxist states. At this convention, the assembly drew from the writings of Bonhoeffer. Since violence and military force were being adopted by the government in support of an unjust policy, can a Christian join this military, they asked? This was a central question for this 1973 Resolution, which agreed that there existed a Divine mandate upon governments to be a servant for good, but when the state betrays its responsibility by engaging in oppression of its citizens, echoing Bonhoeffer, they declared it was better to obey God rather than man.

These four church leaders brought their own unique histories of wayfinding with Dietrich Bonhoeffer. Let's look at their biographies in brief, to illuminate some of the ways they encountered Bonhoeffer and brought his legacy to bear in their struggle against apartheid.

Beyers Naudé

Beyers Naudé (1915–2004) was the prodigy of an elite, Afrikaner nationalist family, whose very identity and formative years were shaped by zeal for the *volk* and the Dutch Reformed Church (DRC). For the Naudé family in which the father was a founding member of the Afrikaner Broederbond (an exclusive brotherhood

committed to the preservation of Calvinist and Afrikaner nationalism), South Africa was the promised land for the chosen Afrikaner
and no one else. The Boer battles against the British or the Zulu in
the interior were divinely charged encounters for the soul of their
birthright. Ironically, it was these Afrikaner liberation values that
would undergird Naudé's future resistance to Afrikaner nationalism and support of Black liberation.

Oom Bey ("Uncle Bey"), as he became affectionately known
during his years of leadership in the church struggle, departed
from the fundamentalist moorings of his childhood during his
young adult years through multiple influences. One of those came
in 1960 after his ordination as a DRC pastor. He was placed in
an elite Afrikaner congregation nearby the seismic Sharpeville
Massacre, in which sixty-nine unarmed Black and Coloured men,
women, and children were gunned down by police. In the wake
of Sharpeville, Naudé joined the ad hoc convening of the World
Council of Churches, where they planned their response to the
tragedy. From this point forward, Naudé's life began to embody
the spirit of Bonhoeffer, causing Bonhoeffer's dear friend Bethge to
later describe Oom Bey as "South Africa's Bonhoeffer."

In 1963, Naudé organized the publication of *Pro Veritate*, a
new journal aimed at resistance to apartheid. The newspaper alone
was not enough for Naudé; he desired a movement of Christians
more akin to the Confessing Church in Nazi Germany. Next, he
helped gather a new ecumenical body, the Christian Institute, for
which he had a larger vision:

> If I consider the way things are going in our country,
> both in church and government spheres, then it must
> become clear to anyone who has experienced or studied
> the development of the church situation in the German
> Third Reich that there are more and more parallels being
> created between the situation in the former Nazi-Ger-
> many and the current one in South Africa . . . If I think
> on all these and other signs then it is clear to me that the
> time has come for a Bekennende Kirche (a "confessional
> Church") for South Africa . . .[120]

Naudé, much like Bonhoeffer, was willing to leave the beaten path to risk being a faithful witness to the gospel against the tyranny of oppression that confronted his nation.

Allan Boesak

As a Coloured, Reformed minister in the Dutch Reformed Mission Church (DRMC) and a member of the Confessing Circle, Boesak was unique in his contributions to the church struggle in the late 1970s and the 1980s.

Despite the severe challenges early in life, his mother's faith helped build a firm foundation, cultivating a concern in him for the poor, the fatherless, the stranger, and the widow. Like Naudé before him, he first encountered Bonhoeffer through his international travels as a graduate student in the Netherlands.

Boesak was ordained into the DRMC at an early age. The DRMC and its associated seminary were formed specifically for students of mixed race, a move which traces back to the origin story of South African apartheid when, in 1857, the Dutch Reformed Church of South Africa approved "church apartheid" for the establishment of separate meeting houses and separate Holy Communion for different racial groups. In 1881, the Dutch Reformed Mission Church (*ZendingKerk*) of South Africa was subsequently instituted for mixed races (Coloureds), along with Reformed churches for white Europeans, Blacks, and Asians.

The DRMC sent Boesak as a delegate to the 1982 Ottawa Synod of the World Alliance of Reformed Churches (WARC) where he added his prophetic voice to the chorus of those unmasking the hypocrisy of apartheid. There he declared a *status confessionis*, naming apartheid a heresy contrary to the gospel and the Reformed tradition. Recall, it was Bonhoeffer, as one of the lone voices of dissent against Hitler's Third Reich and the "German Christians," who was the first since the 1550 Lutheran Formula of Concord to apply *status confessionis* to his own milieu. In response to Hitler's Aryan laws, Bonhoeffer used the term urgently in "The

Church and the Jewish Question," his first public, explicit act of dissidence toward Hitler's regime.

In 1985, Boesak and Desmond Tutu, with the United Democratic Front, organized a march to bring about the release of Mandela, and this act landed Boesak in prison for one year. Here, in the lonely confines of his prison cell, he reflected on his moment in the struggle against apartheid, even as the resistance and violence around the country reached a fever pitch. Two years after his release, at the Fifth International Bonhoeffer Congress (1988), Boesak in his opening address, "What Dietrich Bonhoeffer Has Meant to Me," looked back to that year in exile. It was during this prison confinement when he "had a desire to go quite specifically back to Bonhoeffer."[121] In addition to the Bible, he asked for a copy of Bethge's magisterial work on the life of Bonhoeffer, reviewing once again the life and writing of one of his great inspirations. Here, he reflected on Bonhoeffer with the bruises of one who had suffered in the fight, much like Bonhoeffer in his own prison cell in Tegel after ten years of church resistance to Nazi oppression. Boesak said he contemplated the potent words of Bonhoeffer: "There are things which are worth fighting for without any compromise whatsoever. And I think that peace and social justice, in other words, Christ, are such things."[122] Boesak's heart was equally stirred by these words from Bonhoeffer: "Open your mouth for the voiceless, speak for those who have no voice, speak for those whose voice cannot be heard."[123] In light of the gravity of these words, Boesak underscored the inescapable force of Bonhoeffer's witness which made it "impossible . . . for anyone to do theology without understanding from the inside the meaning of struggle, the meaning of identification with those who are voiceless."[124]

After Boesak's release in 1986, with the nation in upheaval and international outcry against apartheid at its peak, Boesak continued his work within the Reformed family of churches, organizing unity meetings and marches. The truth of that sentiment resounds from Boesak's own heart as he spoke to the 1988 audience gathered in Amsterdam: "I can only be authentic in my faith, I can only be authentic as a theologian in South Africa if I am willing to take my belief from the pulpit or out of my study where I theorize about those things onto the streets where the witness for the Lordship of Jesus Christ must be seen. And I must do that, because this very saying in Bonhoeffer reminds me that if I am not willing to take up my cross and be a disciple of Jesus Christ and pay the price, then I might as well forget to be a theologian or to be a Christian."

Manas Buthelezi

The Rev. Dr. Manas Buthelezi (1935–2016) is considered the father of South African Black theology. Born in 1935 in the Kwa-Zulu Natal province to a large Christian family with nine children, he was ordained in the Evangelical Lutheran Church in Southern Africa's southeastern region. Like his contemporaries, Naudé and Boesak, Buthelezi traveled abroad for further training; his own sojourn led him into the United States where he completed a master's of theology at Yale School of Divinity and a doctorate from Drew University in New Jersey. At age thirty-two, he was the first Black South African to obtain a doctoral degree in theology. It was here that we find the first evidence of Bonhoeffer's wayfinding influence upon Buthelezi. In his doctoral dissertation, *Creation and the Church: A Study in Ecclesiology with Special Reference to a Younger Church Milieu,* Buthelezi draws from Bonhoeffer's own dissertation, *Sanctorum Communio,* as well as *Creation and Fall* and the posthumous collection *Letters and Papers from Prison.*

Buthelezi had his political baptism in 1973 when Naudé asked him to take the post as national regional director of the Christian Institute, where Buthelezi was encouraged to take the institute beyond the abilities of white leadership, exercising Black consciousness for the benefit of apartheid's victims. In 1977, after the violent backlash of the 1976 Soweto Uprising, Buthelezi stood before the Sixth Assembly of the Lutheran World Federation meeting in Dar es Salaam and drew a line in the sand with respect to apartheid. Buthelezi became the first South African to echo Bonhoeffer with his declaration of a *status confessionis.*

Yet, Buthelezi's convictions and example were well-known prior to the watershed events of Soweto. In a provocative *Pro Veritate* essay, "Service to the Down-trodden," he made a clarion call for *all* churches—not just his Evangelical Lutheran tribe, nor just the Black churches—to hear the heart of Jesus found in Matthew 25:31–46. His words again echo the spirit of Bonhoeffer, who learned to see things from the perspective of those below:

> If the church is to render true service to the underdogs of this land, it must be prepared to be maligned, harassed, have its representatives arrested, beaten or even killed if that becomes necessary. There is something wrong in a situation where the church can afford to live in comfort and enjoy social and political respectability while a large portion of its members suffer and enjoy none of those things. That would mean that that church has become irrelevant . . . One has heard talks like: what should the church do for the people of Soweto. The impression created in stating things this way is that the church does not live in Soweto since it has to move in from outside in order to minister to people who are other than itself. Does the church not live *with* the people of Soweto? Has the church deserted the people of Soweto so that it has to reach them from outside? True service includes that the church must not just help the people of Soweto, it must also *become* the people of Soweto, sharing their sufferings and indignities.[125]

In 1972, just prior to his appointment as a regional director of the Christian Institute, Buthelezi traveled to the University of Heidelberg to deliver a lecture at the request of professors, Heinze Eduard Tödt and Dr. Ilse Tödt, who were involved in the Lutheran World Federation's response to apartheid and were close friends of the Bethges. Buthelezi returned three years later, and his presentation once again evoked the evidence of Bonhoeffer's legacy.

In 1973 Buthelezi became the first Black theologian to be banned. Due to his role with the internationally supported Christian Institute and his involvement with the Lutheran World Federation, he had international, ecumenical support. With echoes of the narrative development of Bonhoeffer's own life during the period of growing turmoil and government suspicion toward his activities, Buthelezi was granted an offer to come to the United States in 1974. While in America, he was offered political asylum and scholarships for his children—in other words, a dramatic shift toward a life of relative peace—but, in the spirit of Bonhoeffer who returned to Germany after only twenty-nine days away, he refused.

Desmond Tutu

Desmond Tutu is easily the most known among our church struggle leaders, given his mantle as the Anglican Archbishop of South Africa and the prominent leader of the Truth and Reconciliation Commission (TRC). There are minimal records of Tutu citing the direct influence of Bonhoeffer during the years of his apartheid struggle; yet, there is a thread to follow illustrating his acquaintance and likely reception of Bonhoeffer's witness.

First, we do have a record of Tutu engaging the example of Bonhoeffer from a sermon he delivered at Westminster Abbey in 1975, in which Tutu wondered about the false dichotomy drawn between Bonhoeffer's involvement in the conspiracy against Hitler while Africans were deemed violent insurrectionists for their own resistance to apartheid.[126]

Next, consider Tutu's close relationship with the two aforementioned church struggle leaders Naudé and Boesak. We also know that Tutu was present in Seattle in 1984 for the fiftieth anniversary of the Barmen Declaration.

As well, we have a record of Tutu's words in 1994 looking back upon the years of struggle. While addressing his audience at Emory University, Tutu gave a nod to Bonhoeffer's legacy:

> Hitler purported to be a Christian and saw no contradiction between his Christianity and perpetrating one of history's most dastardly campaigns. What is even more disturbing is that he was supported in this massive crime against humanity by a significant group called "German Christians." Mercifully, there were those like Dietrich

> Bonhoeffer and others who opposed this madness, often
> at great cost to themselves as members of the Confessing
> Church . . . Apartheid in South Africa was perpetrated
> not by pagans but by those who regarded themselves as
> devout Christians.[127]

The costly reconciliation that was part and parcel of Bonhoeffer's writing and witness is much akin to the principle that Tutu fought to engender in the unprecedented reconciliation process for the entire South African people. As the nation crossed out of the wasteland of apartheid, Mandela appointed Archbishop Tutu to pioneer an unprecedented path of healing. In 1995, seventeen persons were named to the TRC, with Tutu receiving the mantle of chairman. The TRC began its work on December 16, 1995, tasked with hearing the confessions of politically derived atrocities from the period of 1960–1994. The TRC would go on, over the course of three years, to hear the testimony of 2,400 victims, receiving a total of 21,519 victim statements connected to 30,384 acts of violence.

Tutu knew that true peace and justice are only attained through the costly reconciliation wrought by the crucifixion of God incarnate. Tutu writes, "We can never give up on anyone because our God was one who had a particularly soft sport for sinners. The Good Shepherd in the parable Jesus told had been quite ready to leave ninety-nine perfectly well-behaved sheep in the wilderness to look for . . . the troublesome, obstreperous old ram."[128]

Tutu believed healing and freedom lie not on the other side of retributive justice, nor on the other side of blanket amnesty, but through a rigorous and painful journey of costly love for enemies—pursuing restorative justice rooted uniquely in the Christian vision of reconciliation. Along with this view of reconciliation, Tutu carried the African philosophy of *ubuntu*. The word is difficult to translate to English, but Tutu describes it this way: "My humanity is caught up, is inextricably bound up, in yours."[129] Out of this ubuntu anthropology, Tutu could conclude: "What dehumanizes you inexorably dehumanizes me."[130] In short, we could say *ubuntu* is inextricably bound up in the notion of community, responsibility, and the inherent dignity of every human (made in *imago Dei*). Once again, we see a kinship between Bonhoeffer and Tutu; they took seriously the notion of Christian responsibility for neighbor, and the sociality of Christ and the church. To answer Bonhoeffer's guiding question, "Who is Jesus Christ for us today?" is inextricably bound up in being a church, Tutu would agree, that "exists for others."

THE WAYFINDING LEGACY OF BONHOEFFER IN SOUTH AFRICA

In his seminal essay from 1942, "After Ten Years," Bonhoeffer looked back upon a decade of confession, dissent, pastoral, and ethical agony over the tragic era of Nazi occupation, and he asked, "Are we still of any use?" In closing, we will offer a response to his inquiry. Was Bonhoeffer a wayfinder for the South African church in their struggle against apartheid?

His own commitment to the church—to the unity, fellowship, and credibility of Christ existing in other persons on earth—and the church's this-worldly "vicarious representative action" (in German, *stellvertretung*) paved the way for him to be an important interlocutor for the South African church's witness amidst injustice.

In that same 1942 essay, Bonhoeffer also asked "Who stands fast?" Success and failure were not his litmus test, but rather faithful allegiance to Christ, for he believed the only one who stands fast against the antichrist tide of unjust rule is the one "whose final standard is not his reason, his principles, his conscience, his freedom, or his virtue, but who is ready to sacrifice all this when he is called to obedient and responsible action in faith and in exclusive allegiance to God—the responsible man, who tries to make his whole life an answer to the question and call of God. Where are these responsible people?"[131] Without a doubt, Naudé, Boesak, Buthelezi, and Tutu all sacrificed to give exclusive allegiance to God; they stood fast as "responsible people" in their own "today."

Bonhoeffer, who grew up with all the privileges one could desire in German society, concluded his reflective essay with these words: "There remains an experience of incomparable value. We have for once learnt to see the great events of world history from below, from the perspective of the outcast, the suspects, the maltreated, the powerless, the oppressed, the reviled—in short, from the perspective of those who suffer."[132] Indeed, each of our church struggle leaders—while diverse in racial, economic, and ecclesial heritage—made the kenotic, Christ-like move in this Bonhoefferian trajectory toward the oppressed. Like Bonhoeffer, they held a perspective "from below." Refusing the luxuries of the theological academy or ecclesiastical vestiges, they made the intentional move to identify with the oppressed, and like Jesus Christ, to suffer with those who suffer in order that they may be free.

On April 25, 1999 at the French Cathedral in Berlin, Bonhoeffer's dear friend and post-mortem biographer, Eberhard Bethge, sat with Archbishop Desmond Tutu in an extraordinary moment where two eras of church struggle merged. Tutu accepted the Dietrich Bonhoeffer Prize on behalf of the South African TRC. The message was clear: Bonhoeffer's church struggle and South Africa's church struggle were one in spirit.

So, was Bonhoeffer "any use" for the South African church? It really is a remarkable story. In Christ, the dividing wall comes down and the white Lutheran pastor in Germany becomes a wayfinder for Black, Coloured, and Afrikaner church leaders at the southern tip of Africa.

WAYFINDING CUES

- Christians from different cultures in faraway lands and past eras offer spiritual resources for our own situation.

- When our neighbors are suffering, indifference is not an option. Christians take responsibility for their neighbors and stand fast against injustice.

- Some ideologies like apartheid are not merely bad "options" on a political spectrum, but rather are a sin, a false gospel, and heresy that threaten to weaken the witness of the church.

- There is only one gospel; false gospels appear in every age.

- Beware of the false gospels of Christian nationalism and racism that threaten allegiance to the kingdom of Christ.

- We must prophetically name the false gospels and evil ideologies that tempt the church.

- The struggle against evil requires our wholehearted attention, activity, and alliance with other Christians.

WAYFINDING QUESTIONS

1. What do you notice about the individuals and churches who took a stand against apartheid? What actions brought change to the apartheid state?

2. Bonhoeffer influenced a variety of individuals in the South African struggle—theologians, pastors, activists—who took different forms of action based on his witness. From what you know of Bonhoeffer's life and theology, what are your reactions to their reception of Bonhoeffer's legacy for their context?

3. In what ways did Bonhoeffer function as a "true witness" for church struggle leaders in South Africa by pointing beyond himself to Jesus Christ?

DEEP WAYFINDING

1. How did Bonhoeffer influence South African churches to adopt theology and action from the perspective of those "from below"? What is the invitation or challenge for you to imitate the Way of Jesus with a perspective "from below"? How might that unfold in your actual life? What habits or relationships might need to form or change?

2. What evils, injustices, or disrepair in the church or in society might Christ be calling you to face with confession and resistance? With whom will you partner?

Acknowledgments

IT GOES WITHOUT SAYING that a book like *Wayfinding with Dietrich Bonhoeffer* takes time to ripen and only emerges whole out of many interactions with friends, family, colleagues, and students. In our case that includes the Life Together House community. Life Together House is a Christian community committed to revitalizing the church for a world wide awake. A "world wide awake" is our term that is deeply indebted to Dietrich Bonhoeffer's "world come of age" phrase, which he coined to describe the radically changing culture he was engaging in the middle twentieth century. Though in a very different time period, Life Together House is similarly wrestling with the profound cultural change occurring today and what it means for the church.

The creative people of Life Together House are working hard to create original content to fulfill our purpose of reinvigorating the people of God in the twenty-first century. *Wayfinding with Dietrich Bonhoeffer* is one example of the original content we are producing. We do pray that wayfinders like Dietrich Bonhoeffer will be a voice who breathe new life into the church today.

With that in mind, there are some specific people we would like to thank. The Wine Cellar Bible Study received the first verbal draft of this book and gave strong encouragement to write it down. Thanks as well to the early adopters who attended our first wayfinding seminar on Bonhoeffer and strengthened the book concept with their many pertinent questions, as well as our guest speaker and author of *Bonhoeffer's Black Jesus*, Reggie Williams. It was during preparation for this seminar—when we were struggling with what to name it—that in a moment of inspiration Jonathan suggested the term *wayfinding*, a term taken from the world of city planning.

Joe also wants to mention the college group from CU Church, especially the irrepressible Demarius Smith and the always thoughtful Wyatt Schlabach, for wayfinding with Dietrich Bonhoeffer and offering many cogent comments. And finally, a special thanks to Joe's daughter Mae, who worked as his research assistant during a critical stage of the book project.

Jonathan would also like to thank his graduate thesis advisory committee—Teresa Ann Barnes, Todd Daly, and Joe Thomas—who encouraged his writing and reflections on Bonhoeffer. As well, he would like to thank J. R. Woodward and Anna Robinson who provided needed insight and encouragement to pursue writing a book for publication. Finally, Jonathan would like to thank his wife, Amber, for affording the space to invest the extra time with his co-author and friend Joe.

Finally, we would like to thank Cascade Books and our editor Rodney Clapp for seeing something special in our book proposal and taking us on as new authors.

Appendix

A Brief Biography
of Dietrich Bonhoeffer

EARLY LIFE

DIETRICH BONHOEFFER (1906–1945) WAS reared in an exceptional German family during the first half of the twentieth century. His father was the chair of psychiatry and neurology at Berlin University and one of his older brothers worked under Albert Einstein. His mother brought a strong Christian influence into the home, having been educated by Moravian Christians.

A fine pianist, a natural leader, and gifted student, Bonhoeffer completed his doctorate in his early twenties. The title of his dissertation was *Sanctorum Communio*. Already Bonhoeffer's thinking was marked by the significance of Christian community in the life of the believer. The Christian life, he wrote, must be marked by a "love for others" since that was the core of Christ's life and teachings.

Bonhoeffer arrived in the United States for a year of study at the beginning of the Great Depression. Spending a year at Union Theological Seminary—a theologically liberal seminary caught up in the Modernist-Fundamentalist feud of the early twentieth century—sharpened Bonhoeffer's appreciation for the centrality of the Scriptures in Christian life. While in New York City, he also became a faithful attendee at Abyssinian Baptist Church, an influential African American church in Harlem. His experience of Black theology and worship would stay with him for the rest of his life.

For his return home to Germany he brought back recorded Black spirituals and played them for his seminary students at Finkenwalde, an experience they failed to appreciate. But more importantly, his experience of a highly segregated American society gave him a unique capacity to see the early Nazi treatment of the Jews for the significant problem that it was, a problem almost every other German pastor and churchman missed. Indeed, his older brother Karl-Friedrich, who had spent time living in the US, wrote Dietrich that he didn't see an analogous situation between the United States and Germany at that time (before Hitler took power), and he even ventured that "our Jewish question is a joke by comparison; there won't be many people who claim they are oppressed here [in Germany]."[133] How things would change.

Bonhoeffer returned to Germany with one more lesson, one he had been thinking about for a long time. How should a Christian respond to war or even social and political oppression? He was deeply moved by the reports he heard about Gandhi, who was using a new nonviolent method to influence the British to leave India peaceably. Bonhoeffer even went so far as to secure an invitation from Gandhi to come and visit him. The meeting never took place because of the rapid pace of events overtaking Germany during the 1920s and 1930s.

However, while at Union Theological Seminary he had befriended a French pacifist by the name of Jean Lasserre, who made the simple but profound argument that on the battlefields of Europe—and remember the First World War was still a fresh memory—Christians should not take up arms against other Christians. Both Lasserre's pacifist arguments and Gandhi's example played a significant role in Bonhoeffer's initial response to the rule of Adolf Hitler.

A Brief Biography of Dietrich Bonhoeffer

The world changed for Germany, and for Bonhoeffer, in 1933 when Adolf Hitler became the leader of the German people. From the beginning, Bonhoeffer had a clear sense of the direction in which Hitler and the Nazis wanted to take the German nation and the German people. In this he had few, if any, fellow workers who shared his prophetic insight.

BEING CHRISTIAN IN NAZI GERMANY

"You'll see the day, ten years from now, when Adolf Hitler will occupy precisely the same position in Germany that Jesus Christ has now."[134]

—REINHARD HEYDRICH,
HIGH RANKING NAZI OFFICIAL,
AND A LEADING ARCHITECT OF THE HOLOCAUST

"[T]he Nazi regime intended eventually to destroy Christianity in Germany, if it could, and substitute the old paganism of the early tribal Germanic gods and the new paganism of the Nazi extremists."[135]

—WILLIAM SHIRER,
THE RISE AND FALL OF THE THIRD REICH

"The question is really: Christianity or Germanism? And the sooner the conflict is revealed in the clear light of day the better."[136]

—DIETRICH BONHOEFFER

So how bad did it get? The first years of the Nazi regime saw the German army, teachers, and most every other German civil servant, including the clergy, swear a personal oath of loyalty and obedience to Adolf Hitler. The Catholic Church signed a concordat with Hitler which virtually guaranteed its silence if he agreed not to meddle in its internal church politics.

How did this happen?

First, Hitler kept his promise during the 1930s to restore Germany to economic greatness and remove the shame of defeat from the aftermath of the First World War. Nationalist Germans, including many Christians, welcomed Hitler as someone who could rebuild the ruins of German culture. The Reverend Martin Niemoller, who later joined the Confessing Church, believed at first that the Fuehrer would bring about a revival in German morality.

Second, Germans were fearful of the rising Red menace to the east. The growing might of the Soviet Union alarmed everyone, including the other Western democracies, and a strong Germany was seen as a necessary bulwark to the communist threat.

But underneath the political and economic successes there brewed a dark underworld of demonic activity. The goal of creating a Thousand Year Reich for the Aryan master race meant that those deemed imperfect must be "removed" from society. The first to be put to death—in what was called the T-4 program—were those who were physically disabled or suffering from mental disorders. The Nazis referred to them as "useless eaters."

The Nazi scientists and doctors were not acting in a vacuum but were part of an international eugenics movement. The idea of preventing the weak in society from reproducing was quite popular and scientifically acceptable in the first half of the twentieth century. In the United States, one eugenics organization awarded prizes for Christian ministers who gave the best sermons on eugenics. County fairs held competitions to determine the winner of "Fitter Family" contests.

After the war, Nazi scientists at the Nuremberg trials pointed to eugenics work in California as inspiration for their actions. While eugenics work in the United States did not include rounding up "undesirables" and killing them, forced sterilizations and other procedures certainly set horrifying precedents. One is reminded of the verse in Luke 12:3: "What you have said in the dark will be heard in the daylight, and what you have whispered in the ear in the inner rooms will be proclaimed from the roofs!" What the American eugenics movement was doing quietly, the Nazi's broadcast from the rooftops.

The capstone of this Aryan master race ideology was the radical anti-Jewishness of the Nazis. Like a tightening noose, the rights and privileges of German citizens of Jewish descent were slowly stripped away during the middle years of the 1930s. Because of family connections, Bonhoeffer was in the know from the beginning about the worst actions of the Nazi regime. The "Aryan Clause" would make it personal for him. The "Aryan Clause" stated that Jews could no longer be part of the German Civil Service, and by extension could not hold an ecclesiastical office in the German church. Bonhoeffer's best friend was a Jewish-Christian pastor, and his twin sister was married to a baptized Jew. The Nazis began to strip the Christian church in Germany of its Jewish roots.

Dr. Hans Kerrl, minister for church affairs, declared in 1935 that Christianity does not consist "in faith in Christ as the Son of God. That makes me laugh . . . No, True Christianity is not dependent upon the Apostles Creed . . . True Christianity is represented by the party, and the German people are now called by the party and especially by the Fuhrer to a real Christianity . . . The Fuhrer is the herald of a new revelation."[137]

Under the Nazis, the church became divided between those known as "German Christians"—who followed Nazi ideology but wanted to keep the outward forms of the Christian church—and the Confessing Church, made up of those committed to the historic Christian faith. Bonhoeffer would be an original member of the Confessing Church. As early as 1934 sides had been chosen within the Christian church of Germany. It was in this context that Bonhoeffer attempted to first pursue a path of nonviolent direct action against the Nazi government before turning to join a small group of highly placed Germans planning to assassinate Adolf Hitler.

THE END

If one happened to have crossed Dietrich Bonhoeffer's path in 1935, it would not have been inconceivable to picture him someday as a German Gandhi. Bonhoeffer was young, brilliant, filled with boundless energy, a pacifist, committed to Jesus' Sermon on the Mount, dedicated to the marginalized everywhere, and diametrically opposed to Adolf Hitler and his Nazi regime. Hence, the utter dismay one experiences when it is discovered that Bonhoeffer's brief, but quite accomplished life ended at the end of a rope as part of a conspiracy to assassinate Adolf Hitler.

First Response

The theological foundation for Bonhoeffer's stance of nonviolent resistance was based on Matthew 5. Bonhoeffer was deep in study and writing on the Sermon on the Mount during his years overseeing the underground Finkenwalde Seminary. He later published this work as *Discipleship* (1937). He wrote:

> By refusing to pay back the enemy in his own coin, and by preferring to suffer without resistance, the Christian exhibits the sinfulness of contumely and insult.[138]

> Nevertheless, "the shameful assault, the deed of violence and the act of exploitation are still evil. The disciple must realize this, and bear witness to it as Jesus did, just because this is the only way evil can be met and overcome."[139]

Back in 1935 Bonhoeffer had written a letter to his brother Karl-Friedrich saying, "I would only achieve true inner clarity and honesty by really starting to take the Sermon on the Mount seriously. Here alone lies the force that can blow all this hocus-pocus sky-high—like fireworks."[140]

Bonhoeffer called his fellow German pastors to bear witness to the abuse of Nazi power in two ways: one, through their privileged position to speak directly to the people, and two, by refusing to obey the Nazis in such a concrete way that the people could not fail to recognize the gross injustices being done. As always, he led the way. He publicly protested through "election flyers . . . , verbal and written communiqués protesting euthanasia and persecution of the Jews, memoranda to convince high-placed officials, even Hitler, to alter course."[141] And he tried to organize pastors to read resolutions from the pulpit, refuse to baptize, wed, and marry, and as one, unified pastoral group publicly leave meetings in protest. This might entail physical abuse or even death for the pastors. Bonhoeffer had recognized this possibility at the outset of his book on discipleship when he stated plainly, "When Christ calls a man, he bids him come and die."[142] Bonhoeffer worked under no illusion that this path would not be costly. He spelled out in straightforward words that the life of following the Jewish Christ in Nazi Germany demanded a costly grace, a grace which cost Jesus his life. Everything else, every other compromise to Nazi ideology, fell into the category of cheap grace, which was no grace at all.

Unfortunately, this was too much for German pastors. The leading theologian Karl Barth urged restraint when it came to responding to the "Aryan Clause." Barth urged Bonhoeffer to wait for "a still more central point" on which to base Christian opposition to the Reich.[143] The Confessing Church's nonresponse demonstrated the dilemma the newly established church body faced. It most directly opposed the "German Christian" and the harm it brought to the Protestant Church in Germany. But to confront the "German Christians" was in reality to challenge the Nazi state—which was the established political authority—something the leadership of the Confessing Church was unable to do based on its own theological understanding of the "two spheres" doctrine.

At a conference in Denmark, Bonhoeffer responded to the lack of action on the part of the German clergy by saying, "Must we be put to shame by non-Christian people in the East?"—a direct reference to Gandhi and the Indian nonviolent resistance to the British.[144]

The turning point for Bonhoeffer came on November 9, 1938. The Nazis dubbed this "Crystal Night" as they terrorized the Jews, smashing their shops, burning their synagogues, and beating them as police officers idly sat by. The Confessing Church remained silent the next day and the days that followed "Crystal Night."

Bonhoeffer underlined two verses from Psalm 74: "They are burning all the houses of God in the land," and "No prophet speaks any longer." He put the date of "Crystal Night" beside the two verses.

"Crystal Night" revealed the other glaring weakness in the Confessing Church's DNA: its primary reason for existence was self-preservation.

Bonhoeffer subsequently distanced himself from the Confessing Church and began to draw closer to his family and a life of subterfuge. His transition came at the same time as the Nazi regime began to crack down on his activities as a pastor, teacher, and author. Beginning in 1937 he was prohibited from teaching at the University of Berlin. One year later, the seminary at Finkenwalde was forcibly closed. And by 1941, it was neither legal for him to speak publicly nor publish any of his writings.

Second Response

In 1939, Bonhoeffer effectively rejoined his family and became part of a conspiracy to assassinate Adolf Hitler.

Through family connections he joined the *Abwehr* (Military Intelligence)—which included many people who opposed Hitler, such as Bonhoeffer's brother-in-law, Hans von Dohnányi. This gave him the official cover he needed for his new work. His new activities now included becoming part of an assassination plot against Hitler, helping Jews escape Germany, and continuing to use his contacts in England to persuade Churchill to recognize officially the leaders of a coup d'état if it took place in Germany. Bonhoeffer had come to believe that only the German military possessed the power to remove Adolf Hitler and the Nazi regime.

As always, Bonhoeffer attempted to work through his actions intellectually and look for theological footing. The difficulty of the moment for Bonhoeffer was captured in his essay "After Ten Years":

> [O]ne may ask whether there have ever before in human history been people with so little ground under their feet—people to whom every available alternative seemed equally intolerable, repugnant, and futile . . .[145]

He worked out his dramatic turn from a passive resistance approach to joining an assassination plot in his book *Ethics*. He argued that in extraordinary circumstances the responsible Christian may sometimes have to take guilt upon his hands if he is to love his neighbor:

> When a man takes guilt upon himself in responsibility, and no responsible man can avoid this, he imputes this guilt to himself and to no one else; he answers for it; he accepts responsibility for it. He does not do this in the insolent presumptuousness of his own power, but he does it in the knowledge that this liberty is forced upon him and that in this liberty he is dependent on grace. Before other men the man of free responsibility is justified by necessity; before himself he is acquitted by his conscience; but before God he hopes only for mercy.[146]

CONCLUSION

"This is the end but for me also the beginning of life."[147]

—DIETRICH BONHOEFFER,
EXECUTION ON APRIL 9, 1945

Unfortunately, the several attempts made on Hitler's life were unsuccessful, including the two attempts by Bonhoeffer's group of conspirators. Bonhoeffer was eventually arrested, imprisoned, and had his life put to an end a few short weeks before the allies liberated his prison camp.

To those who criticize Bonhoeffer's involvement in the assassination plot, his good friend Eberhard Bethge responds, "[H]ow could confessing purists theologically justify your inaction and non-resistance, when you have already become accomplices of criminals."[148]

In Bonhoeffer's last known letter to Bethge, in August 1944 he is found wrestling with the meaning of existence:

> Given that the earth was found worthy to bear the man Jesus Christ, and given that such a man as Jesus Christ once lived, then and only then does our life as human

beings have meaning. Had Jesus not lived, our life would be—in spite of all the other men and women we know and revere and love—meaningless.[149]

Our last report about Bonhoeffer reveals a man facing death with the same kind of confidence and certitude in God that he had demonstrated in living. It is reported that his final words were "This is the end—for me, the beginning of life."[150] The camp doctor at Flossenburg Prison informs us:

> I was most deeply moved by the way this lovable man prayed, so devout and so certain that God heard his prayer. At the place of execution, he again said a short prayer and then climbed the steps to the gallows, brave and composed . . . In the almost fifty years that I worked as a doctor, I have hardly ever seen a man die so entirely submissive to the will of God.[151]

Endnotes

1. Bonhoeffer, *Life Together*, 1954, 23.
2. This chapter first appeared as an article by Joseph L. Thomas in *Touchstone* magazine. It is reformatted here with the permission of *Touchstone*.
3. Bonhoeffer, "Letter to Karl Friedrich," DBWE 13, 285.
4. Bonhoeffer, "The Church and the Peoples of the World," DBWE 13, 307.
5. Bonhoeffer, *No Rusty Swords*, 139.
6. Bonhoeffer, "On the Question of Church Communion," DBWE 14, 675.
7. Bonhoeffer, "Letter to Erwin Sutz," DBWE 13, 135.
8. Bonhoeffer, Editor's Introduction, DBWE 5, 11.
9. Guha, *Gandhi*, 470.
10. Guha, *Gandhi*, 471.
11. Guha, *Gandhi*, 471.
12. Bonhoeffer, "Letter to Erwin Sutz," DBWE 13, 136.
13. Bonhoeffer, "Letter to Erwin Sutz," DBWE 13, 218.
14. Bonhoeffer, "Letter to Erwin Sutz," DBWE 13, 135.
15. Bonhoeffer, "Letter to Elisabeth Zinn," DBWE 14, 134.
16. Kelly and Nelson, *Testament to Freedom*, 463.
17. Bonhoeffer, "Letter to Erwin Sutz," DBWE 12, 101.
18. Kelly and Nelson, *Testament to Freedom*, 463.
19. Bonhoeffer, *Life Together*, DBWE 5, 27.
20. Kelly and Nelson, *Testament to Freedom*, 457.
21. Kelly and Nelson, *Testament to Freedom*, 437.
22. Pangritz, *Polyphony of Life*, 14.
23. Bonhoeffer, "Thoughts on the Day of Baptism," DBWE 8, 390.
24. Bonhoeffer, *Ethics*, DBWE 5, 144–45.
25. Bonhoeffer, *Life Together*, DBWE 5, 27.
26. Bonhoeffer, "Address at The International Youth Conference in Gland," DBWE 11, 379.
27. Bonhoeffer, "Letter to Elisabeth Zinn," DBWE 14, 134.
28. Bethge, *Dietrich Bonhoeffer*, 153.

29. Bonhoeffer, "Sermon on 2 Corinthians 5:10," DBWE 13, 330–331.
30. Bethge, *Dietrich Bonhoeffer*, 154.
31. Bonhoeffer, "Letter to Elisabeth Zinn," DBWE 14, 134.
32. Bonhoeffer, "Letter to Elisabeth Zinn," DBWE 14, 134.
33. Luther, *Three Treatises*, 277.
34. Bonhoeffer, "Letter to Rudiger Schleicher," DBWE 14, 167.
35. Bonhoeffer, "Letter to Eberhard Bethge," DBWE 8, 365.
36. Bonhoeffer, Afterword, DBWE 3, 156.
37. Bonhoeffer, *Life Together*, DBWE 5, 32.
38. Bonhoeffer, *Creation and Fall*, DBWE 3, 23.
39. Kelly and Nelson, *Testament to Freedom*, 463.
40. Kelly and Nelson, *Testament to Freedom*, 463.
41. Bonhoeffer, *Life Together*, DBWE 5, 63.
42. Bonhoeffer, "Letter to Erwin Sutz," DBWE 13, 101.
43. Weber, *Dietrich Bonhoeffer*, 71.
44. Haynes, *Bonhoeffer Phenomenon*, 90–93.
45. Bonhoeffer, "Letter to Winfried Krause," DBWE 16, 347.
46. Bonhoeffer, "Letter to Ernst Wolf," DBWE 16, 359.
47. Bonhoeffer, "Letter to Eberhard Bethge," DBWE 8, 430.
48. Bonhoeffer, *Creation and Fall*, DBWE 3, 23.
49. Bonhoeffer, "Letter to Rudiger Schleicher," DBWE 14, 169.
50. Bonhoeffer, *Life Together*, DBWE 5, 32.
51. Bonhoeffer, *Creation and Fall*, DBWE 3, 25.
52. "German Military Oaths," https://encyclopedia.ushmm.org/content/en/article/german-military-oaths.
53. Bonhoeffer, "Letter from Ruth von Kleist-Retzow," DBWE 15, 173.
54. Bonhoeffer, "American Diary," DBWE 15, 218.
55. Bonhoeffer, "American Diary," DBWE 15, 218.
56. Bonhoeffer, "American Diary," DBWE 15, 218–219.
57. Bonhoeffer, "American Diary," DBWE 15, 221.
58. Bonhoeffer, "American Diary," DBWE 15, 222.
59. Bonhoeffer, "American Diary," DBWE 15, 222.
60. Bonhoeffer, "American Diary," DBWE 15, 223.
61. Bonhoeffer, "American Diary," DBWE 15, 224.
62. Bonhoeffer, "American Diary," DBWE 15, 225.
63. Bonhoeffer, "American Diary," DBWE 15, 225.
64. Bonhoeffer, "American Diary," DBWE 15, 227.
65. Bonhoeffer, "American Diary," DBWE 15, 227.
66. Bonhoeffer, "American Diary," DBWE 15, 228.
67. Bonhoeffer, "American Diary," DBWE 15, 230.
68. Bonhoeffer, "American Diary," DBWE 15, 232.
69. Bonhoeffer, "American Diary," DBWE 15, 232.
70. Bonhoeffer, "Letter from Paul Lehmann," DBWE 15, 205.
71. Bonhoeffer, "Letter from Paul Lehmann," DBWE 15, 205.
72. Bonhoeffer, "Letter from Paul Lehmann," DBWE 15, 205.

73. Bonhoeffer, "American Diary," DBWE 15, 237.
74. Bonhoeffer, "American Diary," DBWE 15, 237.
75. Bonhoeffer, "American Diary," DBWE 15, 237.
76. Bonhoeffer, "American Diary," DBWE 15, 253–254.
77. Bonhoeffer, "American Diary," DBWE 15, 237.
78. Bonhoeffer, "Letter to Reinhold Niebuhr," DBWE 15, 210.
79. Bonhoeffer, *Letters and Papers from Prison*, 3.
80. Bonhoeffer, "Church and the Jewish Question," DBWE 12, 365–66.
81. Bonhoeffer, *Cost of Discipleship*, 2018, 142.
82. Rasmussen and Bethge, *Dietrich Bonhoeffer*, 47–50.
83. Kelly and Nelson, *Testament to Freedom*, 104.
84. Shirer, *Rise and Fall of the Third Reich*, 167.
85. Shirer, *Rise and Fall of the Third Reich*, 238–239.
86. Wind, *Dietrich Bonhoeffer*, 85.
87. Bonhoeffer, *Ethics*, DBWE 6, 113–114.
88. Kelly and Nelson, *Testament to Freedom*, 399.
89. Metaxas, *Bonhoeffer*, 404.
90. Schlingensiepen, *Dietrich Bonhoeffer*, 262.
91. Dramm, *Dietrich Bonhoeffer and the Resistance*, 34–35.
92. Dramm, *Dietrich Bonhoeffer and the Resistance*, 83.
93. Dramm, *Dietrich Bonhoeffer and the Resistance*, 42.
94. Bethge, *Dietrich Bonhoeffer*, 625.
95. Bethge, *Dietrich Bonhoeffer*, 604.
96. Leibholz-Bonhoeffer, *Bonhoeffers*, 188.
97. Bonhoeffer, "Letter to Eberhard Bethge, April 30, 1944," DBWE 8, 362.
98. Bonhoeffer, "Letter to Eberhard Bethge, April 30, 1944," DBWE 8, 362.
99. Bonhoeffer, "Letter to Eberhard Bethge, June 8, 1944," DBWE 8, 425–26.
100. Bonhoeffer, "Letter to Eberhard Bethge, June 8, 1944," DBWE 8, 366.
101. Bonhoeffer, "Letter to Eberhard Bethge, June 8, 1944," DBWE 8, 427.
102. Bonhoeffer, "Letter to Eberhard Bethge, June 8, 1944," DBWE 8, 405.
103. Bonhoeffer, "Letter to Eberhard Bethge, June 8, 1944," DBWE 8, 426–27.
104. Bonhoeffer, "Letter to Eberhard Bethge, June 8, 1944," DBWE 8, 427.
105. Bonhoeffer, "Thoughts on the Day of Baptism," DBWE 8, 390.
106. Bonhoeffer, "Letter to Eberhard Bethge, May 5, 1944," DBWE 8, 73.
107. Bonhoeffer, "Letter to Eberhard Bethge, May 5, 1944," DBWE 8, 447.
108. Bonhoeffer, "Letter to Eberhard Bethge, May 5, 1944," DBWE 8, 451.
109. Bonhoeffer, "Letter to Eberhard Bethge, May 5, 1944," DBWE 8, 534.
110. Bonhoeffer, "Letter to Eberhard Bethge, May 5, 1944," DBWE 8, 534.
111. Bonhoeffer, "Editors Introduction," DBWE 8, 27.
112. Bonhoeffer, "Outline for a Book," DBWE 8, 503.
113. Bonhoeffer, *Ethics*, DBWE 6, 139.
114. Bonhoeffer, *Ethics*, DBWE 6, 144–45.
115. Bonhoeffer, Prologue, DBWE 8, 52.
116. Thompson, *History of South Afrika*, 186.
117. Mandela, *Struggle is My Life*, 191.

118. Moodie, *Rise of Afrikanerdom*, 1.
119. Bethge, *Bonhoeffer: Exile and Martyr*, 39.
120. Naudé, "Tyd vir 'n 'Belydende Kerk' is Daar," 1, 4, 6.
121. Boesak, "What Dietrich Bonhoeffer Has Meant to Me," *Bonhoeffer's Ethics*, 21–29.
122. Boesak, "What Dietrich Bonhoeffer Has Meant to Me," 23.
123. Boesak, "What Dietrich Bonhoeffer Has Meant to Me," 23.
124. Boesak, "What Dietrich Bonhoeffer Has Meant to Me," 23.
125. Buthelezi, "Service to the Down-trodden," 8.
126. Haynes, *Bonhoeffer Phenomenon*, 63.
127. Tutu, "Desmond & Leah Tutu Legacy Foundation and the Legacy of Dietrich Bonhoeffer."
128. Tutu, *No Future without Forgiveness*, 84.
129. Tutu, *No Future without Forgiveness*, 31.
130. Tutu, *No Future without Forgiveness*, 31.
131. Bonhoeffer, "After Ten Years," in *Letters and Papers* 1997, 5.
132. Bonhoeffer, "After Ten Years," in *Letters and Papers* 1997, 17.
133. Bethge, *Dietrich Bonhoeffer*, 110.
134. Metaxas, *Bonhoeffer*, 166.
135. Shirer, *Rise and Fall of the Third Reich*, 240.
136. Bethge, *Dietrich Bonhoeffer*, 232.
137. Shirer, *Rise and Fall of the Third Reich*, 238–39.
138. Bonhoeffer, *Cost of Discipleship*, 142.
139. Bonhoeffer, *Cost of Discipleship*, 142.
140. Bonhoeffer, "Letter to Karl Friedrich," DBWE 13, 284–85.
141. Rasmussen, *Bonhoeffer*, 129–30.
142. Bonhoeffer, *Cost of Discipleship*, 44.
143. Bethge, *Dietrich Bonhoeffer*, 239.
144. Bonhoeffer, "Speech at Fano Conference," DBWE 13, 309.
145. Bonhoeffer, *Letters and Papers from Prison* (1972), 3.
146. Bonhoeffer, *Ethics*, DBWE 6, 282–83.
147. Bethge, *Bonhoeffer: Exile and Martyr*, 96.
148. Bethge, *Dietrich Bonhoeffer*, 9.
149. Bonhoeffer, *Reflections on the Bible*, 104.
150. Schlingensiepen, *Dietrich Bonhoeffer*, 378.
151. Metaxas, *Bonhoeffer*, 237.

Bibliography

Bethge, Eberhard. *Dietrich Bonhoeffer: A Biography.* New York: HarperCollins, 1977.

———. *Bonhoeffer: Exile and Martyr.* New York: Seabury, 1975.

Boesak, Allan. "What Dietrich Bonhoeffer Has Meant to Me." In *Bonhoeffer's Ethics: Old Europe and New Frontiers,* edited by G. Carter, R. Van Eyden, H. D. Van Hoogstraten, and J. Wiersma, 21–29. Kampen, The Netherlands: Kok Pharos, 1991.

Bonhoeffer, Dietrich. *Berlin: 1932–1933.* Edited by Larry L. Rasmussen. Translated by Isabel Best, David Higgins, and Douglas W. Stott. DBWE 12. Minneapolis: Fortress, 2009.

———. *Conspiracy and Imprisonment 1940–1954.* Edited by Mark Brocker. Translated by Lisa E. Dahill. DBWE 16. Minneapolis: Fortress, 2016.

———. *The Cost of Discipleship.* London: SCM, 2001.

———. *The Cost of Discipleship.* New York: Touchstone, 2018.

———. *Creation and Fall.* Edited by John W. de Gruchy. Translated by Douglas Stephen Bax. DBWE 3. Minneapolis: Fortress, 1997.

———. *Ecumenical, Academic, and Pastoral Work: 1931–1932.* Edited by Victoria J. Barnett, Mark Brocker, and Michael B. Lukens. Translated by Isabel Best, Nicholas S. Humphrey, Marion Pauck, Anne Schmidt-Lange, and Douglas W. Stott. DBWE 11. Minneapolis: Fortress, 2012.

———. *Ethics.* Edited by Eberhard Bethge. New York: MacMillan, 1986.

———. *Ethics.* Edited by Clifford J. Green. Translated by Reinhard Krauss, Douglas W. Stott, and Charles C. West. DBWE 6. Minneapolis: Fortress, 2008.

———. *Letters and Papers from Prison.* New York: Macmillan, 1972.

———. *Letters and Papers from Prison.* New York: Touchstone, 1997.

———. *Letters and Papers from Prison.* Edited by Geffrey B. Kelly. Translated by Daniel W. Bloesch. DBWE 8. Minneapolis: Fortress, 2004.

———. *Life Together.* New York: Harper & Row, 1954.

———. *Life Together and Prayerbook of the Bible.* Edited by Geffrey B. Kelly. Translated by Daniel W. Bloesch. DBWE 5. Minneapolis: Fortress, 2004.

Bibliography

———. *London 1933–1935*. Edited by Keith W. Clements. Translated by Isabel Best. DBWE 13. Minneapolis: Fortress, 2007.

———. *No Rusty Swords: Letters, Lectures and Notes, 1928–1936*. New York: Harper and Row, 1965.

———. *Reflections on the Bible, Human Word and Word of God*. Edited by Manfred Weber. Peabody, MA: Hendrickson, 2004.

———. *Theological Education at Finkenwalde: 1935–1937*. Edited by H. Gaylon Barker and Mark Brocker. Translated by Douglas W. Stott. DBWE 14. Minneapolis: Fortress, 2013.

———. *Theological Education Underground: 1937–1940*. Edited by Victoria J. Barnett. Translated by Claudia D. Bergmann, Peter Frick, and Scott A. Moore. DBWE 15. Minneapolis: Fortress, 2011.

Buthelezi, Manas. "Service to the Down-trodden." *Pro Veritate* 16.2 (June 1977) 8.

de Gruchy, John W. *Dietrich Bonhoeffer: Witness to Jesus Christ*. Minneapolis: Fortress, 1987.

de Gruchy, John W., and Steve de Gruchy. *The Church Struggle in South Africa, Twenty-fifth Anniversary Edition*. Minneapolis: Fortress, 2005.

Dramm, Sabine. *Dietrich Bonhoeffer and the Resistance*. Minneapolis: Fortress, 2009.

"German Military Oaths." https://encyclopedia.ushmm.org/content/en/article/german-military-oaths.

Guha, Ramachandra. *Gandhi: The Years that Changed the World, 1914–1948*. New York: Knopf Doubleday, 2018.

Haynes, Stephen R. *The Bonhoeffer Phenomenon: Portraits of a Protestant Saint*. Minneapolis: Fortress, 2004.

Kelly, Geffrey B. and F. Burton Nelson, eds. *A Testament to Freedom: The Essential Writings of Dietrich Bonhoeffer*. San Francisco: HarperCollins, 1990.

Leibholz-Bonhoeffer , Sabine. *The Bonhoeffers: Portrait of a Family*. New York: St. Martin's, 1971.

Luther, Martin. *Three Treatises*. Minneapolis: Fortress, 1970.

Mandela, Nelson. *The Struggle is My Life: His Speeches and Writings Brought Together with Historical Documents and Accounts by Fellow Prisoners*. London: IDAF, 1990.

Metaxas, Eric. *Bonhoeffer: Pastor, Martyr, Prophet, Spy*. Nashville: Thomas Nelson, 2010.

Moodie, T. Dunbar. *The Rise of Afrikanerdom: Power, Apartheid and the Afrikaner Civil Religion*. Berkeley: University of California Press, 1975.

Naudé, Beyers. "Die Tyd vir 'n 'Belydende Kerk' is Daar." *Pro Veritate*, 4.3 (July 1965) 1–6. Translated by Dietloff van der Berg, via email, February 16, 2020.

Pangritz, Andreas. *The Polyphony of Life: Bonhoeffer's Theology of Music*. Edited by John W. de Gruchy and John Morris. Translated by Robert Steiner. Eugene, OR: Cascade, 2019.

Bibliography

Rasmussen, Larry L. *Bonhoeffer: Reality and Resistance*. Louisville: Westminster John Knox, 2005.

Rasmussen, Larry, and Renate Bethge. *Dietrich Bonhoeffer: His Significance for North Americans*. Eugene, OR: Wipf & Stock, 1990.

Schlingensiepen, Ferdinand. *Dietrich Bonhoeffer, 1906–1945: Martyr, Thinker, Man of Resistance*. New York: Bloomsbury T. & T. Clark, 2010.

Shirer, William. *The Rise and Fall of the Third Reich: A History of Nazi Germany*. London: Secker and Warburg, 1960.

Thompson, Leonard. *The History of South Afrika*. New Haven: Yale University Press, 2000.

Tutu, Desmond. "The Desmond & Leah Tutu Legacy Foundation and the Legacy of Dietrich Bonhoeffer." March 1, 2020. https://www.tutu.org. za/the-desmond-leah-tutu-legacy-foundation-and-the-legacy-of-dietrichbonhoeffer/.

———. *No Future without Forgiveness*. New York: Doubleday, 1999.

Weber, Manfred. *Dietrich Bonhoeffer: Reflections on the Bible, Human Word and Word of God*. Peabody, MA: Hendrickson, 2004.

Wind, Renate. *Dietrich Bonhoeffer: A Spoke in the Wheel*. Grand Rapids: Eerdmans, 1992.